THE NEW BIBLE CURE
for OSTEOPOROSIS

DON COLBERT, MD

SILOAM
A STRANG COMPANY

Most STRANG COMMUNICATIONS BOOK GROUP products are available at special quantity discounts for bulk purchase for sales promotions, premiums, fund-raising, and educational needs. For details, write Strang Communications Book Group, 600 Rinehart Road, Lake Mary, Florida 32746, or telephone (407) 333-0600.

THE NEW BIBLE CURE FOR OSTEOPOROSIS by Don Colbert, MD
Published by Siloam
A Strang Company
600 Rinehart Road
Lake Mary, Florida 32746
www.strangbookgroup.com

Design Director: Bill Johnson
Cover design by Amanda Potter

Library of Congress Cataloging in Publication:
Colbert, Don.
  The new Bible cure for osteoporosis / by Don Colbert.
     p. cm.
  Includes bibliographical references.

ISBN 978-1-59979-757-1

1. Osteoporosis--Popular works. 2. Osteoporosis--Religious aspects--Christianity. I. Title.

RC931.O73C635 2009

616.7'16--dc22

2009028253

Portions of this book were previously published as *The Bible Cure for Osteoporosis* by Siloam, ISBN 978-0-88419-681-5, copyright © 2000.

09 10 11 12 13 — 9 8 7 6 5 4 3 2 1

Printed in the United States of America

CONTENTS

INTRODUCTION
A BRAND-NEW BIBLE CURE
FOR A BRAND-NEW YOU! 1

A Bold, New Approach.. 2

1 WISE UP TO WIN..5

The Shrinking of America.. 6

Straight Talk About Osteoporosis 7

Understanding Bone Health and Bone Loss.......... 8

The Bone Renewal Process 9

Two Types of Bones.. 11

Why Do Bones Weaken? 12

The role of digestion 12

The role of stress 13

The role of hormones 13

Risk Factors for Osteoporosis.............................. 14

Women 14

Anyone 14

Warning Signs 16

Fractures... 16

Pain... 17

Loss of height... 17

Dowager's hump or worsening scoliosis............. 18

Compressed organs.. 18

Shortness of breath 18

Dental problems 18

Osteopenia and Early Detection of
Osteoporosis.. 18

Diagnosing Osteoporosis 20

Take a Positive Look Ahead 22

2 POWER UP WITH NUTRITION 25

Make Sure You're Consuming the Right
Amount of Calcium.. 26

Foods That Rob You of Calcium 30

Magnesium-rich Foods: A Cornucopia
of Choices.. 33

Eat Foods Rich in Vitamin D 35

Check Your Blood Level of Vitamin D 38

A Path to Healthy Bones: Nutritional Steps
for Preventing Osteoporosis................................. 39

1. Put aside excess protein. 39

2. Reduce the intake of carbonated drinks......... 39

3. Get a grip on the effects of excess
sugar and caffeine. 40

4. Finesse your fiber intake................................. 40

5. Understand acidic foods and their role. 40

6. Decrease the salt. 44

7. Decrease or avoid alcohol. 44

8. Favor fruit. 44

9. Why lemon and lime water? 46

10. Enjoy chlorophyll foods and their benefit. 46

11. Watch out for aluminum. 46

Osteoporosis, American Style 46

Tips for Healthy Eating 47

God's Help 48

3 CHARGE UP WITH EXERCISE 51

Benefiting Bones With Exercise 51

Get Moving! 52

Weight-Bearing Exercises 53

Getting Started 54

Overhead presses 54

Lunges 55

Squats 55

Push-ups 56

A Final Word About Weight Control 57

Changing the Future 59

4 BUILD UP WITH VITAMINS
AND SUPPLEMENTS 63

Significant Supplements... 63

A good multivitamin 63

Calcium.. 64

Vitamin D... 65

Magnesium.. 66

Other Important Nutrients for Strong Bones...... 68

Vitamin K$_2$... 68

The B vitamin family 69

Boron.. 70

Strontium... 70

Silicon 71

Medications for Osteoporosis.............................. 71

Bisphosphonates.. 72

Hormones... 73

Other medications 76

Confusion Over Calcium Supplements................. 77

Calcium carbonate.. 79

Calcium citrate 79

Cal apatite (microcrystalline hydroxyapatite)...... 80

It's Up to You 83

5 LOOK UP WITH DYNAMIC FAITH 87

Another Dimension... 87

Cheer Up 88

Persecution Strikes to the Bone............................ 89

Less Stress.. 90

A Troubled Soul 91

Joy Stealers 92

    Drainers 92

    Irritators... 92

    Changers 93

    Circumstances 93

    Contentment 93

Breaking the Power of Negative Emotions.......... 94

Accent the Positive!... 94

Take These Bible Cure Steps 95

    1. Resist worry. 95

    2. Pray.. 95

    3. Trust in God's Word to heal and sustain you. 96

    4. Start smiling. 97

    5. Start laughing.. 97

CONCLUSION
    BEGIN A BRAND-NEW LIFE—TODAY!........99

A PERSONAL NOTE From Don Colbert 101

APPENDIX
    NUTRITIONAL SUPPLEMENTS FOR
    OSTEOPOROSIS 103

NOTES 105

A BRAND-NEW BIBLE CURE
FOR A BRAND-NEW YOU!

THE BIBLE SAYS that God is in the business of protecting your bones! Does that sound odd to you? Well, Psalm 34 says precisely, "Many are the afflictions of the righteous, but the LORD delivers him out of them all. He guards [protects] all his bones; not one of them is broken" (vv. 19–20, NKJV).

God never intended for you to experience the pain of bone degeneration from osteoporosis or to suffer from a single break or fracture. In fact, this little book contains a powerful plan to help you overcome this painful, degenerative process.

Through His divine wisdom, God has provided foods and powerful substances that will help prevent or stop the progression of osteoporosis in your body. In addition, He has blessed you with the power of faith to overcome the challenges that assault your body and your mind. Hosea 4:6 says, "My people are destroyed for lack of knowledge" (NKJV). This Bible Cure book is designed to provide the wisdom and knowledge to understand how to use both the natural and divine resources that God has made available to you to defeat the threat of osteoporosis in your life—forever!

God does not purpose for you to grow old hurting and degenerating. In fact, His plan and purpose for your life is ongoing strength and renewal. In the Bible, you can read His blessing for your life:

> Let all that I am praise the LORD; with my whole heart, I will praise his holy name. Let all that I am praise the LORD; may I never forget the good things he does for me. He forgives all my sins and heals all my diseases. He redeems me from death and crowns me with love and tender mercies. He fills my life with good things. My youth is renewed like the eagle's!
>
> —PSALM 103:1–5

A BOLD, NEW APPROACH

I have good news for you: osteoporosis is not your destined end in old age. With God's grace and wisdom, health and joy await you! I have helped hundreds of patients reverse osteoporosis by treating them with the same methods you are about to discover.

I have taken the confusion away from osteoporosis and instead have made it simple and easy to understand. Throughout this book I will share practical steps you can take to overcome osteoporosis through natural methods of good nutrition, vitamins, supplements, lifestyle changes, and exercise. I will also provide you with faith-building scriptures and Bible Cure prayers to empower you to overcome osteoporosis spiritually.

As you read this book, prepare to win the battle against osteoporosis. You will begin to feel better physically, emotionally, and spiritually. This Bible Cure book is filled with hope, encouragement, and valuable information on how to stay fit and develop a healthy lifestyle that reduces your risk of developing osteoporosis later in life. You'll also learn what you can do to slow its progression, stop it, or even reverse it if you have already been diagnosed with the disease.

Originally published as *The Bible Cure for Osteoporosis* in 2000, *The New Bible Cure for Osteoporosis* has been revised and updated with the latest medical research on osteoporosis. If you compare it side by side with the previous edition, you'll see that it's also larger, allowing me to expand greatly upon the information provided in the previous edition, providing you with a deeper understanding of what you face and how to overcome it.

Unchanged from the previous edition are the timeless, life-changing, and healing scriptures throughout this book that will strengthen and encourage your spirit and soul. As you read, apply, and trust God's promises, you will also find powerful Bible Cure prayers to help you line up your thoughts and feelings with God's plan of divine health for you—a plan that includes living victoriously.

Another change since the original *Bible Cure for Osteoporosis* was published is that I've released a book called *The Seven Pillars of Health.* I encourage you to read it because the principles of health it contains are the foundation to healthy living that will affect all areas of your life. It sets the stage for everything you will ever read in any other book I've published—including this one.

With that, I welcome you to *The New Bible Cure for Osteoporosis.* You can confidently take the natural and spiritual steps outlined in this book to walk a steady path without the pain and suffering of osteoporosis. It is my prayer that these practical suggestions for health, nutrition, and fitness will bring wholeness to your life—body, soul, and spirit. May they deepen your fellowship with God and strengthen your ability to worship and serve Him.

—DON COLBERT, MD

A **BIBLE CURE** Prayer for You

Almighty God, You are my strength. Give me wisdom and knowledge so that I may apply all that I learn in this book and thereby overcome osteoporosis. Thank You for the awesome gift of the temple of my body. Fill me with the joy and confidence to praise You for victory over osteoporosis even when I experience pain. Heal me with Your Word. Guide me in the pathway of Your healing for my life. Amen.

1

WISE UP TO WIN

ACCORDING TO GOD's Word, your bones can be so healthy and strong that they actually rejoice! The Bible says, "All my bones shall say, 'LORD, who is like You, delivering the poor from him who is too strong for him, yes, the poor and the needy from him who plunders him?'" (Ps. 35:10, NKJV).

Now, it's doubtful that the psalmist was suggesting that a person's bones could actually speak. But he certainly was implying that a person's bones could feel great when God heals them.

The first Bible Cure step for experiencing healing and health for your bones is gaining understanding. The more you understand this disease, the better equipped you will be to defeat it. God does not leave us ignorant or helpless when facing obstacles in life. He has graced us with the knowledge we need to live healthy, vital lives.

As you grow in knowledge and understanding of osteoporosis, this is my prayer for you taken from the Bible: "Dear friend, I hope all is well with you and that you are as healthy in body as you are strong in spirit" (3 John 2).

You also need to be aware of the many ways God has provided to care for your temple—which is what the Bible calls your body. "Don't you realize that your body is the temple of the Holy Spirit, who lives in you and was given to you by God? You do not belong to yourself, for God bought you with a high price. So you must honor God with your body" (1 Cor. 6:19–20). You see, caring for your body is more important than you may have thought. God wants you to care for your temple so that you can live a happy, joyful, and healthy life serving God.

THE SHRINKING OF AMERICA

A few years ago, I conducted a physical exam on a sixty-five-year-old woman named Jane. She was a thin blonde with a fair complexion, sporting high-heeled shoes and a bouffant-style hairdo.

Jane had not had a physical exam for over ten years and was very concerned when my nurse told her she was only five feet four inches tall. She insisted that she was five feet eight inches tall. Even though her high heels and high hairdo made her appear tall, she was really only five feet four inches barefoot.

Jane indeed had shrunk four inches in the ten years since her last physical exam. Although she had no back pain, dowager's hump, scoliosis, bone pain, or any other symptoms of osteoporosis, after finishing her physical exam, I sent Jane for a DEXA (dual-energy X-ray absorptiometry) scan, which revealed that she had severe osteoporosis.

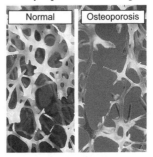

However, Jane's story has a happy ending. With a good nutrition and exercise program, we were able to reverse her osteoporosis in only a couple of years without any medications.

© 2009 International Osteoporosis Foundation

A **Bible Cure** *Health Fact*
Gravity and Your Bones

Astronauts have been found to be at risk of accelerated bone loss due to prolonged weightlessness while they are in space, leading researchers to conclude that you need gravity for strong, healthy bones.[1]

Straight Talk About Osteoporosis

Osteoporosis—which means "porous bones"—is a progressive loss of bone mass that leads to decreased bone density. Just how prevalent is it? I'm afraid osteoporosis is increasing at an alarming rate in the United States. When I originally published *The Bible Cure for Osteoporosis* in 2000, the latest research at that time showed that about 20 million Americans had osteoporosis. Now, just a decade later, with the release of this revised and expanded edition of the book, I'm sorry to report that approximately 44 million Americans have osteoporosis or low bone mass, 68 percent of whom are women.[2]

Many people think that only women need to worry about developing osteoporosis. However, over two million American men also suffer from osteoporosis. Approximately one out of every two women and one out of every four men age fifty and older will have an osteoporosis-related fracture in their lifetime.[3] When these osteoporosis-related fractures occur in the hip, they are life-threatening for both men and women, so it is very important to start improving your bone health today!

Another misconception is that osteoporosis is for the elderly.

However, osteoporosis can strike at any age. I have treated patients in their thirties with osteoporosis.

The bones most commonly affected by this disease include the hips, spine, ribs, and forearms. In fact, osteoporosis is responsible for over 1.5 million fractures yearly, including seven hundred thousand vertebral fractures, three hundred thousand hip fractures, two hundred fifty thousand wrist fractures, and over three hundred thousand fractures of other sites in the body. The estimated national direct expenditure for osteoporosis-related fractures is approximately $14 billion each year.[4]

UNDERSTANDING BONE HEALTH AND BONE LOSS

Bone loss actually begins to increase after age forty, and it greatly accelerates in postmenopausal women. Like many women, you may have thought that you did not need to worry about osteoporosis until after you have reached menopause. However, menopause is only one factor in the development of this disease.

I recently treated a thirty-four-year-old woman with severe osteopenia, the stage right before osteoporosis in which a significant amount of bone loss occurs. Even though she was only thirty-four years old, had plenty of estrogen, and was taking calcium supplements, she already had bone loss. So, you see, it's critically important that you begin implementing these principles while you are young—if possible—before you have experienced any degree of bone loss. A major key to overcoming the threat of osteoporosis throughout your entire lifetime is prevention.

A **Bible Cure** *Health Fact*
The Importance of Calcium

Your body will actually cannibalize your bones by taking calcium out of the bones in order to maintain a stable calcium level in the blood and cells.

The Bone Renewal Process

To prevent and overcome osteoporosis, you first need to understand how your bones mature, develop, and then begin to lose mass in midlife. Your bones are composed of approximately 70 percent mineral salts and 30 percent protein matrix.[5] The protein matrix is mainly composed of collagen fibers, chondroitin sulfates, and hyaluronic acid.

Calcium salts are the most essential element of bone formation, and 99 percent of the calcium in your body is stored in your bones. Only about 1 percent of your total calcium is in your blood and inside your cells.[6]

Calcium phosphate is a mineral salt that is present in the protein matrix and provides strength to the bone. The calcium and phosphate form crystals that are bound to the proteins and are arranged in an orderly pattern and called hydroxyapatite.

To understand this better, imagine a sidewalk made of iron rebar. The iron rebar is like the cross-links of proteins of collagen, and the concrete surrounding the rebar is similar to the hydroxyapatite crystals composed of mainly calcium and phosphorus. Now you are beginning to get the picture. Concrete without rebar is not nearly as strong as concrete with rebar, and it is the same with our bones. They must have this strong collagen protein as well as hydroxyapatite surrounding them.

Many people think that once our bones are formed, they remain the same forever. However, our bones are made of living tissue that is continually being renewed throughout our lives. Let me explain this bone renewal process to you.

> I pray that from his glorious, unlimited resources he will empower you with inner strength through his Spirit. Then Christ will make his home in your hearts as you trust in him. Your roots will grow down into God's love and keep you strong. And may you have the power to understand, as all God's people should, how wide, how long, how high, and how deep his love is. May you experience the love of Christ, though it is too great to understand fully. Then you will be made complete with all the fullness of life and power that comes from God.
>
> —Ephesians 3:16–19

There are two main types of bone cells: osteoclasts and osteoblasts. *Osteoblasts* are cells that build bone and make hydroxyapatite in collagen. The *osteoclasts* are always searching for older bone that needs to be renewed. These cells break down the old bone using enzymes to dissolve collagen as well as hydroxyapatite. They leave behind very small lesions. The osteoblasts then move into these small spaces and produce new bone. Therefore, old bone is being dissolved continuously, and new bone is being formed. This renewal process is called "remodeling." The status of our bones is actually dependent upon the delicate balance of these two processes.

A **BIBLE CURE** *Health Fact*

Dem Bones, Dem Bones

Did you know that through the body's constant "remodeling" process of breaking down and rebuilding bone, the average adult skeleton is completely replaced every ten years?[7]

TWO TYPES OF BONES

Most people picture their bones as a skeleton with hard, dried bones. However, only 75 percent of your skeleton is made of a strong, compact bone called *cortical bone*. This is the main type of bones in your arms, legs, and ribs.[8] It regenerates slowly at about 2 to 3 percent per year.[9]

Your remaining bone mass is *trabecular bone*, a spongy, porous, and lightweight bone with many holes in it. This type of bone is found mainly in the pelvis, hips, and spine, and it regenerates much faster than cortical bone[10] at approximately 25 percent a year.[11] Also, trabecular bone is more prone to osteoporosis.

During growth years, new bone formation dominates, and very little bone is resorbed into the body. From the end of puberty to about age thirty-five, the body maintains a good balance of bone formation and bone resorption. However, after age thirty-five the process of dissolving the bone becomes increasingly dominant. After forty, it actually accelerates, and after menopause, usually around age fifty, it increases even more.

Put another way, bone mass usually reaches its peak when a woman is about thirty-five years old. Between the ages of fifty-five to seventy, women typically experience a 30 to 40 percent loss of bone mass.[12]

Realize that over your lifespan, if you are a woman, you will lose approximately 50 percent of your trabecular bone and 30 percent of your cortical bone. If you are a man, you will lose about 45 percent of your trabecular bone as well as about 15 percent of your cortical bone.[13]

WHY DO BONES WEAKEN?

As we age, our bodies (particularly our bones) absorb calcium with less and less efficiency. A child usually absorbs 50 to 70 percent of the calcium from his or her food. However, adults may absorb only about 20 to 30 percent of the calcium in their diets, and older adults absorb even less calcium.[14]

As you grow older, this lack of calcium is the single most important factor contributing to the decrease of bone mass and the increased risk of chronic osteoporosis. To understand osteoporosis, it's important for you to realize how much your body needs this vital nutrient. We will discuss practical steps to helping your body get the calcium it needs a little later on.

The role of digestion

After menopause, many women are extremely deficient in hydrochloric acid, which is a stomach acid that aids digestion. Without enough hydrochloric acid in the stomach, calcium carbonate cannot be absorbed efficiently. A woman with a normal amount of hydrochloric acid in her stomach generally absorbs about 22 percent of the calcium in her diet, whereas an individual with a deficiency absorbs only about 4 percent.[15] I will discuss more about this later as well.

> My life is poured out like water, and all my bones are out of joint. My heart is like wax, melting within me.
>
> —PSALM 22:14

The role of stress

Depression, anxiety, and excessive long-term stress are also risk factors for osteoporosis because they are commonly associated with elevated cortisol levels. Cortisol is our body's own cortisone. Realize your body actually produces elevated amounts of cortisol in response to depression, anxiety, and long-term stress.

Physicians have known for decades that long-term use of corticosteroid medications is associated with high risk of osteoporosis. However, a chronic stress state such as anxiety and depression also sets one up for a similar scenario. My books *Stress Less*, *The Bible Cure for Stress*, and *The New Bible Cure for Depression and Anxiety* address this important topic in detail.

The role of hormones

Sex hormones are produced primarily by the ovaries and testes, and as we age, our bodies produce fewer and fewer of them. The rapid decrease of the hormone estrogen in women's bodies during menopause puts them at a greater risk of developing osteoporosis than men, whose hormone levels decrease much more gradually with age. I will discuss more about hormones later in this book, but for now, realize that there is a direct relationship between the lack of estrogen during and after menopause and the development of osteoporosis. Low progesterone levels may also be associated with bone loss, especially in premenopausal females.

RISK FACTORS FOR OSTEOPOROSIS

You are at an increased risk of developing osteoporosis if you have any of the following risk factors. Notice that some risk factors are uncontrollable, such as your gender, ethnicity, and family history. Others are very much under your control, such as your intake of certain nutrients, smoking, and excessive drinking.

Women

- Blonde or redheaded with fair skin
- Caucasian and Asian
- Thin (weighing less than 125 pounds)
- Short stature and small bones
- Postmenopausal
- Never been pregnant
- History of anorexia nervosa, bulimia, or early menopause

Anyone

- Family history of osteoporosis
- Inactivity (a sedentary lifestyle)

- Smoking or excessive alcohol consumption—that means more than one drink a day for women or more than two drinks a day for men
- Excessive physical exercise
- Excessive stress or depression
- Hyperthyroidism
- Hyperparathyroidism
- High homocysteine level
- Gastric or small bowel resection
- Long-term use of corticosteroids (such as prednisone), thyroid medications, and Lupron, which is a medication for endometriosis
- Long-term use of anticoagulant medication such as heparin, which is a blood thinner
- Long-term use of anticonvulsants
- High vitamin A intake
- High animal protein intake
- High sugar intake
- High sodium intake
- Excessive intake of sodas containing phosphoric acid (most do)
- Low calcium intake
- Nutritional deficiencies

A **BIBLE CURE** Health Fact

The Effect of Alcohol on Your Bones

Bone loss and alcohol abuse often go hand in hand. Up to 50 percent of men being treated for alcohol abuse have low bone mass.[16]

WARNING SIGNS

As I mentioned previously, bone mass in women usually reaches its peak around age thirty-five and then begins to decrease. Unfortunately, most women ages thirty-five to sixty-five do not realize they are losing bone mass because bone loss occurs without symptoms. But the osteoporosis that develops as a result of significant bone loss does have several telltale symptoms. They typically occur when the disease has reached an advanced stage and include:

Fractures

This is the wake-up call that most often alerts people that they have developed osteoporosis. Among healthy people, fractures only happen when a serious trauma to the bone has occurred, but in people with osteoporosis, fractures can occur after minor traumas, such as bending over, lifting light objects, coughing, sneezing, bumping into a piece of furniture, or stepping off a curb. Fractures of the rib, compression fractures of the spine, and fractures of the hip are the most common fractures experienced by those with osteoporosis. (Compression fractures of the spine can pinch the spinal nerves, creating chronic pain and eventually leading to hip fractures and fractures of other bones throughout the body.) Also, it is common for people with osteoporosis who break one bone to have recurring fractures of the same bone or to break other bones as well.

Approximately 90 percent of hip fractures happen to people over the age of sixty, and because women are more prone to osteoporosis than men are, they experience the majority of these hip fractures—roughly 80 percent of them. The United States ranks highest in the world with more than three hundred thousand hip fractures per year. Some estimate the number of Americans hospitalized for hip fractures could exceed five hundred thousand by the year 2040.[17]

Any fracture in a person with osteoporosis is serious because bones that are not as dense as they should be do not heal quickly, and sometimes they don't heal completely. But hip fractures are especially serious. They can lead to loss of independence, loss of function, and death.

Pain

Persistent pain in the spine or muscles of the lower back, chronic discomfort or pain in the neck that is not caused by an injury, or pain in the hip are common symptoms of osteoporosis. Nighttime leg cramps and aching or tenderness of the bones are also symptoms.

Loss of height

Some people notice that their clothing doesn't fit the same or that their pants are too long but still don't make the connection to loss of height as a result of bone loss. This is why I recommend getting your height checked yearly. If you are a woman, I strongly encourage you to get an annual physical. Be sure your doctor keeps a chart on your height, measured without shoes.

Dowager's hump or worsening scoliosis

A dowager's hump is an actual hump that develops due to the progressive curvature of the upper back and neck. Stooped posture and back pain can accompany these warning signs.

Compressed organs

As a consequence of compression fractures of the spine, the abdominal organs can become compressed, leading to an enlarging belly, constipation, and weight loss. People may become short-waisted and appear to have a belly or increased folds of skin on their abdomen as compression fractures occur.

Shortness of breath

Because of compression fractures of the thoracic spine, patients may develop shortness of breath since the lungs are not able to fully expand.

Dental problems

Other signs of osteoporosis include periodontal disease and loss of teeth as osteoporosis affects the jawbone.

OSTEOPENIA AND EARLY DETECTION OF OSTEOPOROSIS

You don't have to wait until you are experiencing the symptoms I just described to start monitoring and improving your bone health. Osteoporosis is a progressive disease, and the earlier it is detected, the easier it is to stop and reverse.

Before osteoporosis develops, there is a stage called *osteopenia*, which is defined as having bone density that is lower than average but not low enough to be diagnosed as osteoporosis. It is natural to experience some level of low bone density (osteopenia) as you age, because old bone breaks down faster than new bone is made. But it is possible to slow this progression into osteoporosis and even stop and reverse it, as you will learn throughout this book.

The best way to arm yourself is prevention. If you are young, follow the principles in this book to make your bones as strong as possible now. This will make it less likely that you will experience significant bone loss when you are older.

The next best defense against osteopenia and osteoporosis is early detection. Whether or not you are experiencing any symptoms, if you have any of the risk factors listed previously in this chapter, ask your doctor about a bone density test. The following Bible Cure Health Tip will also give you a good idea of when you should be tested.

A **BIBLE CURE** Health Tip
When Should You Be Tested for Osteoporosis?[18]

The International Society of Densitometry and the National Osteoporosis Foundation have very similar recommendations about when to have a bone density test. They recommend that the following people be tested:

1. Women who are 65 years of age and older

2. Men who are 70 years of age and older

3. Postmenopausal women under age 65 with risk factors such as smoking, weighing less than 125 pounds, and a family history of osteoporosis

4. Adults with a history of a low-trauma fracture (hip, wrist, or spinal fracture from minor trauma)

5. Adults with a health condition associated with low bone density or bone loss (hyperthyroidism, hyperparathyroidism, rheumatoid arthritis, vitamin D deficiency, etc.)

6. Adults taking medications associated with low bone density or bone loss (thyroid hormone medications, seizure medications, excessive doses of corticosteroids, medications that block sex hormone production, etc.)

7. Anyone being treated with drugs for osteoporosis or being recommended for treatment due to evidence of bone loss

8. Anyone whose standard skeletal X-rays show reduced bone density

I usually start screening women for osteopenia and osteoporosis at age fifty, and men around age sixty-five.

DIAGNOSING OSTEOPOROSIS

Standard skeletal X-rays do not always help detect osteoporosis, because bone loss is not visible on an X-ray until you have lost more than 30 percent of your bone mass.[19] Therefore, special tests that use radiology to measure the density of minerals like calcium in your bones have been developed. Bone mineral density (BMD) testing helps your doctor estimate the strength of your bones and predict your chances of experiencing a fracture or other symptom of osteoporosis.

The DEXA scan (dual-energy X-ray absorptiometry) is the most accurate of all bone mineral density tests and therefore is considered the gold standard. Since there may be differences in the bone mineral density in different areas of the body, most doctors request at least two sites be measured—I actually prefer three. Sites that are most commonly tested include the hips, spine, and forearm, with the areas of greatest concern being the hips and spine.

Other tests that measure BMD are peripheral dual-energy X-ray absorptiometry (P-DEXA), dual photon absorptiometry (DPA), ultrasound, and quantitative computed tomography (QCT). These tests vary in accuracy, cost, and levels of radiation exposure.

A **BIBLE CURE** Health Fact
The DEXA Scan

The DEXA scan uses only a very small dose of radiation that is only about 1/30 the dose of a chest X-ray.

After you undergo testing, your bone mineral density is compared to average young adults of the same gender and ethnicity. The difference between your BMD and the average BMD is expressed as a standard deviation (or SD). The SD is your T-score and is either a positive or negative number.

The World Health Organization (WHO) defines osteoporosis as having a T-score of 2.5 or more standard deviations below the average (in other words, a T-score of -2.5 or less).[20] Osteopenia is defined when the T-score is between 1 and 2.5 standard deviations below average (a score of -1 to -2.5). A normal bone density receives a T-score of one standard deviation or less below the average (a score of 0 to -1).

Here's a chart to help simplify it for you:

BONE DENSITY T-SCORES

T-Score	Condition
0.0 to -1.0	Normal Bone Density
-1.0 to -2.5	Osteopenia
-2.5 and lower	Osteoporosis

If your doctor recommends you undergo a DEXA scan, don't worry. A DEXA scan is painless and requires no preparation. If you have osteoporosis, your doctor will probably want to check your DEXA scan each year, and if you have osteopenia, your doctor will probably want to check your DEXA scan approximately every two years.

TAKE A POSITIVE LOOK AHEAD

If you are younger or just approaching midlife, your future health is in your hands. Even if you older or you are experiencing some of the symptoms of osteoporosis, you can combat and even reverse them by understanding this disease.

God has a strong, vital future for you as you walk in His wisdom. This Bible Cure plan for living in divine health can strengthen your bones and empower you to serve Him in body, soul, and spirit.

A **BIBLE CURE** Prayer for You

Lord, You have revealed the causes of osteoporosis. In You are also the remedies, cures, and preventions for this destructive disease. Guide and direct me in applying what I have learned and thereby prevent or overcome osteoporosis in my body. Consecrate my body, soul, and spirit to live in divine health. Amen.

A **BIBLE** **CURE** *Prescription*

Memorize and say aloud this healing word from God:

I am suffering and in pain. Rescue me, O God, by your saving power. Then I will praise God's name with singing, and I will honor him with thanksgiving.
—PSALM 69:29–30

Describe what you learned about how osteoporosis develops:

_____

_____

_____

Write a prayer thanking God for revealing this knowledge about preventing osteoporosis to you:

_____

_____

_____

_____

_____

_____

_____

_____

_____

POWER UP WITH NUTRITION

G OD HAS CREATED the foods that you need to strengthen your bones and provide divine health to your body. These foods have existed from the beginning of time. The Bible reveals:

> Then God said, "Look! I have given you every seed-bearing plant throughout the earth and all the fruit trees for your food. And I have given every green plant as food for all the wild animals, the birds in the sky, and the small animals that scurry along the ground—everything that has life." And that is what happened. Then God looked over all he had made, and he saw that it was very good! And evening passed and morning came, marking the sixth day.
>
> —GENESIS 1:29–31

Decide today to eat right so that you will prevent osteoporosis and arrest any traces of this disease in your body. The best foods from God's creation for you to eat are those rich in calcium and magnesium. Let's explore what they are.

MAKE SURE YOU'RE CONSUMING THE RIGHT AMOUNT OF CALCIUM

We all know that calcium is needed for strong, healthy bones, but how much calcium do you need every day? Here's a simple chart of recommended daily intakes:

DAILY CALCIUM REQUIREMENTS

Age	Milligrams per day
9–18	1,300
19–50	1,000
51 and older	1,200

Dairy products are an excellent source of calcium. An 8-ounce glass of milk (that's just one cup) contains about 300 mg of calcium. It's interesting to note that the fat content of the milk does not change the amount of calcium. In other words, you get the same amount of calcium (300 mg) from *any* 8-ounce glass of milk: fat-free, low-fat, skim, whole, or lactose-free. Because fat-free and low-fat milk contain little or no fat, I recommend drinking organic varieties of these two kinds of milk to add calcium to your diet without adding extra fat.

Most other dairy products, such as yogurt, cheese, and buttermilk, also contain high amounts of calcium. I recommend organic low-fat or skim milk dairy products. Some of my favorite dairy products are plain, organic kefir and yogurt, which are actually much healthier sources of calcium than fruit-flavored, sugar-sweetened yogurt products and tend to be less acid-generating than other forms of dairy. They also make a great alternative if you are sensitive to dairy. Other options for dairy that I highly recommend are organic low-fat goat's milk, goat's-milk yogurt, goat's-milk kefir, or low-fat goat's-milk cheese.

However, I do need to caution you about going overboard. Even though dairy products are high in calcium, excessive intake of dairy such as milk and cheese will usually create an acidic environment in your tissues. Realize that milk lacks magnesium and potassium and causes greater excretion of urea from the kidneys, which may lead to loss of calcium, magnesium, and potassium. The proteins in milk, including casein and whey, add to your body's acidic burden. This is one of the reasons I believe it is important not to consume excessive amounts of dairy and to be sure to balance your dairy consumption with plenty of vegetables, seeds, and nuts, which contain generous amounts of potassium and magnesium.

A BIBLE CURE *Health Fact*

Milk: Does It Really Do a Body Good?

It is interesting to note that the countries with the highest rates of osteoporosis—including the United States, England, and Sweden—also consume the most milk, whereas China and Japan eat less protein and dairy and have much lower rates of osteoporosis. Why? One reason is that milk and other dairy products contain only very small amounts of magnesium. Without adequate magnesium, the body only absorbs about 25 percent of the calcium content in the milk.

Unfortunately, some Americans are allergic to dairy or are lactose intolerant, and they will need to consume other dietary sources of calcium. Small amounts of calcium are found in many foods, but there are only a few foods that contain large quantities of this vital mineral. Vegetables such as broccoli, cauliflower, peas, and beans are high in calcium. In addition, nuts—including Brazil nuts, hazelnuts, and almonds—and seeds, such as sunflower seeds, contain high amounts of calcium. Here's a chart to show you some of the nondairy foods with the highest amounts of calcium:

Nondairy Dietary Sources of Calcium[1]	
Sardines, canned in oil, with bones	3 ounces contain 324 mg of calcium
Salmon, pink, canned, solids with bone	3 ounces contain 181 mg of calcium
Spinach, cooked	½ cup contains 120 mg of calcium
Turnip greens, boiled	½ cup contains 99 mg of calcium
Kale, cooked	1 cup contains about 94 mg of calcium
Kale, raw	1 cup contains about 90 mg of calcium
Chinese cabbage, raw	1 cup contains about 74 mg of calcium
Broccoli, raw	½ cup contains 21 mg of calcium
Bread, whole-wheat	1 slice contains 20 mg of calcium
Almonds	1 ounce (about 22 nuts) contains 75 mg of calcium

What foods do I recommend that are high in calcium and will help strengthen your bones? Well, organic God-made foods, instead of man-made foods, are always the best foods. Here's a short list of general recommendations:

- Organic and processed seasonal whole foods such as dark green leafy vegetables including collard greens, broccoli, mustard greens, watercress, bok choy, parsley, endive, and chicory are loaded with calcium, for example. Bok choy has 790 mg of calcium per 100 calories.

- Nuts and seeds including sesame seeds, sunflower seeds, pumpkin seeds, flaxseeds, hemp seeds, Brazil nuts, walnuts, and pecans are also good sources of calcium. For example, a quarter cup of sesame seeds has 351 mg of calcium.

- Beans and legumes including chickpeas, lentils, black beans, kidney beans, lima beans, mung beans, and peas are fairly good sources of calcium.

- Sea vegetables such as dulse, wakane, arame, etc. are mineral rich and contain magnesium, calcium, and many trace minerals that also help to protect our bones.

- Fruits are typically very alkalinizing to the body and help to protect the bones and also generally contain magnesium and potassium, which help to buffer the organic acids produced in the body. Citrus fruit including oranges, grapefruits, limes, and lemons are high in vitamin C, which helps to improve the absorption of calcium. It is important to choose organic fruit and preferably fruit that is in season. I also recommend eating the whole fruit whenever possible over drinking fruit juice.

- Whole grains contain vitamins and minerals and also help to maintain bone strength. However, use wheat bran in moderation and not when taking calcium supplements, since excessive amounts can interfere with calcium absorption. Also, taking fiber supplements with calcium may decrease the absorption of calcium.

A **BIBLE CURE** Health Fact
Antacid Warning

Most antacids contain calcium carbonate, but some also contain aluminum, a toxic heavy metal. Aluminum interferes with calcium absorption.

FOODS THAT ROB YOU OF CALCIUM

Do you drink a lot of carbonated beverages and eat a lot of red meat? These foods contain high amounts of phosphorus, which decreases bone calcium. It's no wonder we are experiencing an epidemic of osteoporosis in the United States since the consumption of these items is so high. Eating large quantities of red meat will almost certainly cause a loss of calcium from your bones and increase your risk of osteoporosis. Allow me to go into more detail about the dangers of the typical American diet.

The standard American diet is very acid forming, making those who consume it more prone to bone loss. Processed meats (hot dogs, luncheon meats, pepperoni, etc.), fast foods (burgers, fries, tacos, pizzas, etc.), and other processed foods (canned soups and vegetables) are typically loaded with sodium and contain excessive amounts of protein. Excessive salt intake causes a loss of calcium, as does excessive protein intake. The 2005 Dietary Guidelines for Americans advise limiting sodium intake to 2,300 mg a day, or 1 teaspoon of salt a day.[2]

Also, the standard American diet includes sodas. Most sodas contain phosphoric acid, which increases calcium excretion in the urine, eventually causing us to slowly lose bone. Caffeine present in coffee as well as sodas also leaches calcium from the bones. However, tea—according to studies—does not harm the bones. I recommend my patients choose more water with lemon or lime or unsweetened iced tea, green tea, or white tea.

Another major problem with the standard American diet is excessive animal protein intake. Excess of animal protein contains a lot of acids and phosphorus, which leach calcium from the bones.

Realize that God did not design our bodies to eat large quantities of meat. The human's intestinal tract is about four times longer than a person is tall, which favors plant food ingestion. Compare this to a true carnivore's intestine, which is much shorter and only about two to three times longer than their body.

Also, a carnivore's stomach has approximately four times the amount of hydrochloric acid as an herbivore's stomach. As a result, carnivores are able to digest meat much more rapidly and eliminate waste products more quickly through the shorter GI tract.

Human saliva is alkaline, which helps us digest carbohydrates, whereas the saliva of a carnivore is acidic. Carnivores also have much larger kidneys and livers than humans in order to handle the excessive acids, including uric acid, and nitrogenous waste products as a result of excessive meats.

Several studies have revealed that women who ate less meat and more vegetables had less bone degeneration than their sisters who ate more meat.[3]

For years, I have been writing in my books to eat organic low-fat meats in moderation, which means we do not need meat at every meal. I personally only eat about 3 to 4 ounces of organic and very lean meat once or twice a day, and I also combine whole grains and beans to form complete protein.

Also, sugary foods and beverages, white bread, pasta, white rice, and other processed grains, junk food, and alcohol are acid-producing foods and may leach calcium from the bones. Here are two more cautions I'd like to include:

- Several foods that are high in calcium also contain oxalic acid, which interferes with calcium absorption. There is nothing wrong with eating these foods, but realize that you may not be reaping the benefits of increased calcium intake if you consume them because of the oxalic acid they contain. They include chocolate, spinach, cashews, asparagus, kale, chard, beet greens, and rhubarb.

- Even though soy is high in calcium, the oxalates in soy can bind calcium. Some studies show that soy can cause problems with bone strength, and others show that the right type of soy isoflavones help to protect the bones. Until this controversy is cleared, go easy on soy, and do not drink it or eat it on a daily basis if you have osteoporosis.

MAGNESIUM-RICH FOODS: A CORNUCOPIA OF CHOICES

In addition to storing 99 percent of your body's calcium, your teeth and bones store about 60 percent of its magnesium.[4] Magnesium assists over three hundred different enzyme reactions in your body. Calcium causes muscles to contract, but magnesium enables them to relax. Calcium and magnesium are vitally important in bone health and need to be balanced for optimal bone health. Also, just like calcium, the absorption of magnesium requires vitamin D, and without adequate magnesium, calcium may not be fully utilized.

Magnesium helps your body to absorb calcium from your diet, and it also helps your bones to retain the calcium. Without enough magnesium, you are much more prone to lose bone rapidly. Magnesium is also necessary in order to prevent excess calcium intake from causing calcifications in soft tissues.

However, approximately 56 percent of Americans are not consuming enough magnesium in their diets.[5] Foods highest in magnesium are nuts—such as almonds, walnuts, and cashews—whole grains, seafood, and legumes. I recommend simply eating some extra nuts, whole grains, and legumes in order to add more magnesium to your bone-building program. Other magnesium-rich foods include:

- Apples, apricots, avocados, bananas, cantaloupe, grapefruit
- Soy products
- Brewer's yeast
- Brown rice
- Figs
- Garlic
- Kelp
- Lemons
- Lima beans
- Millet
- Peaches
- Black-eyed peas
- Salmon

Herbs that contain magnesium include alfalfa, bladder wrack, catnip, cayenne, chamomile, chickweed, dandelion, eyebright, fennel seed, hops, lemongrass, licorice, paprika, parsley, peppermint, raspberry leaf, red clover, sage, and yarrow.

You should also avoid or decrease intake of foods that can increase magnesium excretion, such as refined carbohydrates (white bread, white rice, etc.). Eating a diet that is high in fats, proteins, and phosphorus can also decrease your body's magnesium absorption.

Other foods that rob your body of magnesium include:

- Caffeine
- Sugar
- Alcohol
- Soft drinks
- Tea
- Rhubarb
- Spinach
- Cocoa

EAT FOODS RICH IN VITAMIN D

Most people drink milk that's been fortified with vitamin D. However, vitamin D milk and dairy foods can cause magnesium absorption to decrease. Without enough magnesium, the active form of vitamin D in the blood is reduced.

Vitamin D is a fat-soluble vitamin that is actually manufactured in our skin as it comes in contact with the sun's ultraviolet rays. It is found mainly in meat products—especially in fish liver oils. Good dietary sources of vitamin D include egg yolks, butter, cod liver oil, salmon, mackerel, herring, and other meats. Artificial fats, such as olestra, may prevent vitamin D from being absorbed. Also fat-blockers such as chitosan or the new fat-blocking weight-loss drug orlistat (Xenical or Alli) may also decrease absorption of vitamin D.

Vitamin D is required for your body to absorb calcium and phosphorus and to maintain normal levels of calcium and phosphorous in your bloodstream. Vitamin D also helps in bone mineralization. Without adequate vitamin D, bones may become brittle and thin. Vitamin D is very important for the transport of calcium from the intestines into the blood. It also decreases the excretion of calcium from the kidneys and helps the bones mineralize.

I check vitamin D levels on most of my patients, and I would say that about 90 to 95 percent of individuals over fifty are deficient in vitamin D. Dr. John Jacob Cannell, executive director of the Vitamin D Council, says that perhaps 70 percent of the U.S. population has vitamin D_3 levels below 35 ng/mL (nanograms per milliliter).[6] Children who receive insufficient amounts of vitamin D can develop rickets, which is a disease that causes the legs to become bowed because the bones are undermineralized.

> God arms me with strength, and he makes my way perfect.... You have armed me with strength for the battle; you have subdued my enemies under my feet.
>
> —PSALM 18:32, 39

For the past forty-plus years, most doctors have been recommending that two to three large glasses of milk be drunk every day, which provides between 600 and 900 mg of calcium. However, as I mentioned in chapter 1, in spite of our high intake of milk and milk products, including ice cream, cheese, and milk, we still have an epidemic of osteoporosis. Drinking milk is not the best way for your body to get necessary vitamin D. Sunlight and eating foods with vitamin D are better sources of vitamin D because they do not inhibit magnesium absorption as does drinking milk.

Our skin makes vitamin D when we are exposed to UVB radiation from the sun. Usually, the daily requirement of vitamin D can be obtained from being in the sunlight for approximately ten to fifteen minutes at midday wearing shorts and a T-shirt. Dark-skinned individuals require approximately five times more sun exposure in order to get the same amount of vitamin D as a fair-skinned person. Because of less exposure to sunshine, people living in northern states are more likely to be deficient in vitamin D.

Very few foods contain any significant amounts of vitamin D naturally (see the following table of selected food sources of vitamin D).

Food Sources of Vitamin D	
Cod liver oil	1 Tbsp contains 1,360 IU of vitamin D
Salmon, cooked	3.5 ounces contain 360 IU of vitamin D
Mackerel, cooked	3.5 ounces contain 345 IU of vitamin D
Tuna	3 ounces contain 200 IU of vitamin D
Sardines	1.75 ounces contain 250 IU of vitamin D
Vitamin D fortified milk	1 cup contains about 98 IU of vitamin D
Whole egg	1 egg contains 20 IU of vitamin D

CHECK YOUR BLOOD LEVEL OF VITAMIN D

The 25-hydroxy vitamin D blood test is a way your doctor can measure how much vitamin D is in your body. Many researchers are now advising adults to achieve a minimum blood level of vitamin D of 30 ng/mL. However, new research recommends that individuals get their vitamin D_3 level to over 50 ng/mL.[7]

If you are at risk of developing osteoporosis or are already suffering from the disease, please ask your physician for a 25-hydroxy vitamin D test or a 25-OHD3 test. Most doctors unfortunately still do not perform this very important blood test. However, it is imperative to get your vitamin D level in the optimal range in order to reverse osteoporosis.

A **BIBLE CURE** Health Tip
Red Yeast Rice

Red yeast rice (RYR) is rice fermented by a strain of red yeast. It is native to China and has been used in Chinese medicine for centuries. Additionally, it has long been used in Chinese cuisine as a natural food coloring agent.

RYR contains a compound that is identical to lovastatin, a drug that lowers cholesterol.[8] However, certain strains of red yeast rice contain a type of phytonutrient called monacolins, which increase bone formation. Not all red yeast rice strains have these monacolins, but studies have shown that certain strains of red yeast rice could actually increase bone density in osteoporotic bone.[9]

At the time of this book's printing, red yeast rice is used to lower cholesterol in the United States, but it is hard to find in the form needed for bone health. In the future I hope it will also be available to treat osteoporosis.

I always recommend taking coenzyme Q_{10}—at least 100 mg a day—if you take any red yeast rice supplement.

A Path to Healthy Bones: Nutritional Steps for Preventing Osteoporosis

I recommend that you follow these guidelines to help insure a future free from the effects of osteoporosis:

1. Put aside excess protein.

As I mentioned earlier in this chapter, high-protein diets, egg whites, casein in milk, and lactalbumin are all associated with an increase in the elimination of calcium in the urine. Casein and lactalbumin are also found in many protein supplements. As the amount of protein in your diet increases, the amount of calcium eliminated from your body also increases.

High-protein diets, such as the Atkins Diet and the South Beach Diet, are very common in the United States. Such diets encourage people to eat very large quantities of meat and should be avoided because they can increase calcium loss, setting the stage for osteopenia and osteoporosis. I believe that the popularity of such diets is contributing to the high incidence of osteoporosis in this country.

2. Reduce the intake of carbonated drinks.

Remember, soft drinks contain high levels of phosphorus. When phosphorus levels in the blood are high, calcium levels tend to decline. Therefore, the body compensates by pulling calcium out of the bones to raise these calcium levels. Do you know why soft drinks contain high levels of phosphates? Because this chemical helps to dissolve the enormous amount of sugar contained in most soda pop varieties.

3. Get a grip on the effects of excess sugar and caffeine.

Too much sugar and caffeine in your diet can also cause your body to eliminate calcium. Coffee shops are springing up around the country, despite the fact that coffee contains more caffeine than most other drinks. Americans are drinking more coffee than ever, which is another reason we are seeing such an epidemic of osteoporosis in America.

4. Finesse your fiber intake.

It's important to get enough fiber, but when you are aiming to maximize your body's intake of calcium, it is important to be careful about *when* you eat fiber. Too much fiber consumed at the same time as calcium can inhibit its absorption by the intestines. Therefore, when you eat fiber, either increase the amount of calcium you take with it, or eat the fiber at different times than the calcium to avoid the fiber binding the calcium and thus preventing its absorption.

5. Understand acidic foods and their role.

Your body thrives in an alkaline environment. Most people understand the importance of keeping their swimming pool or their aquarium in the correct pH range. If the water gets either too acidic or too alkaline, it begins to get discolored and eventually will grow algae.

Kidney specialists now recognize that as most Americans age, they live in a chronically low-grade metabolic acidosis or an acidic condition.[10] Realize that if the pH of your urine, which is indicative of the pH of your tissues, becomes chronically acidic, you begin to slowly cannibalize your bones as calcium is leached out of the bones to buffer the acids produced in your body.

Certain minerals are very alkalinizing since they buffer the acids in the body. They include calcium, magnesium, and potassium. However, when our tissues are constantly acidic, we lose valuable minerals and eventually lose bone.

Decrease or avoid highly acidic foods, for they can slowly destroy your bones. The pH value of foods actually measures the level of acidity or alkalinity of fluids in the body. A pH of 7.0 is neutral. Higher than 7.0 is alkaline, and less than 7.0 is acidic.[11] The main fluids of the body include the blood, the saliva, and the urine. The pH of each of these fluids can be tested to determine acidity or alkalinity.

Blood pH

It is vitally important that blood maintain a constant pH of 7.4. If it rises by just 0.1 point acidity from 7.4 to 7.3, you would probably go into a seizure and eventually die.[12] It is so critically important to maintain the blood pH that the body will actually rob the bones—robbing from Peter to pay Paul—in order to keep the blood pH constant at 7.4.

Salivary pH

The pH of your saliva usually indicates the kinds of foods you have eaten. It should be around 6.5. The pH of the stomach is usually very acidic and measures around 1.5 to 3.5 in order to digest your food.[13]

Urinary pH

The pH of urine is the best indicator of acidity in body tissues. A urinary pH of 7.0 to 7.5 is ideal.[14] You might be thinking that 5.0 is only two points away from an ideal pH, but a pH of 5 is actually one hundred times more acidic than a pH of 7!

When an individual's urinary pH is less than 6, acidosis has occurred. This state is present in the majority of Americans. In fact, whenever I check a urinalysis, at least nine out of ten of my patients have a pH of around 5.0.

Acidosis simply means that our bodies are producing too many acids. A high-fat, high-sugar, and high-protein diet creates significant amounts of acid in our bodies, and this is reflected in our urinary pH. Exercising the muscles to fatigue also creates a buildup of lactic acid, which will also be reflected in an acidic urine pH reading.

You can easily determine your own body's pH by purchasing pH paper at your local health food store or pharmacy and periodically checking your own urine. The best time to test your pH is when you get out of bed in the morning. Or you can go to a doctor and have a urinalysis performed.

The pH of our tissues depends on metabolic processes such as breathing and moving and also depends on the foods we eat and the beverages we drink as well as the stress we are under. In other words, the food that you choose to eat and the water that you choose to drink are able to either raise or lower the pH of your urine, which in turn will help to either protect your bones or destroy your bones.

It is no wonder that we are experiencing an epidemic of osteoporosis when most Americans drink coffee, eat bread, cheese, meats, fats, pasta, potatoes, and other acid-producing foods, while avoiding fruits and vegetables, which are alkaline-producing foods.

Acidosis actually slowly cannibalizes a person's bones by causing minerals, especially calcium, to be extracted from them to buffer acids, thus raising the pH of the body.[15] Before the body actually extracts calcium and other minerals from the bones, it typically first attempts to buffer the acids through more rapid breathing, which allows the body to rid itself of the carbon dioxide that causes a buildup of acids.

Your body also uses alkaline amino acids to buffer acids. The kidneys will produce bicarbonates that also buffer acids. Finally, if your body is being overwhelmed by acids that the above mechanisms cannot control, it will actually begin to cannibalize your bones, pulling out phosphates, calcium, magnesium, potassium and other minerals in an emergency attempt to buffer the acids.

> You say, "Food was made for the stomach, and the stomach for food." (This is true, though someday God will do away with both of them.) But you can't say that our bodies were made for sexual immorality. They were made for the Lord, and the Lord cares about our bodies.
>
> —1 CORINTHIANS 6:13

In my practice, I see this daily with patients who are taking in significant amounts of coffee, alcohol, proteins, sugars, starches, and fats. These individuals are overwhelming their bodies' buffering systems, thereby creating severe acidosis, which slowly cannibalizes their bones.

I remember one lady who was forty years old when she suffered a fractured arm and two fractured ribs after falling while getting out of the shower. This lady's diet consisted of large amounts of coffee, soft drinks, sugary foods, high-protein foods, and almost no fruits and vegetables. She also smoked and drank a couple of mixed drinks each night.

This diet created such a condition of acidosis in her body that her bones were cannibalized, and a simple fall while getting out of the shower resulted in three broken bones. I immediately sent her over for a DEXA scan, and the test confirmed that she had developed severe osteoporosis. I believe it was a direct result of her chronic state of acidosis.

6. Decrease the salt.

As I mentioned earlier, excessive salt causes calcium loss. You should limit your daily intake of sodium to 2,300 mg, which is 1 teaspoon of salt per day.

7. Decrease or avoid alcohol.

Drinking excess alcohol, or more than one drink a day for a female and more than two drinks a day for a male, will increase calcium loss. A single drink is 5 ounces of wine.

8. Favor fruit.

Eat alkaline-producing foods. At least 50 percent of your diet should consist of fruits and vegetables, which are alkaline-producing foods.

Even though lemons, limes, oranges, berries, and grapefruit are acidic outside of the body, inside the body they are actually alkalinizing. Alkalinizing foods include any of the following:

Fruit	
Dates	Mangoes
Grapes	Pineapples
Citrus fruits	Raspberries
Apples	Blackberries
Bananas	Apricots
Cherries	Olives
Peaches	Coconuts
Pears	Figs
Plums	Raisins
Papaya	Melons
Grains	
Millet	Sprouted grains
Buckwheat	
Meat and Dairy Products	
Nonfat milk	
Nuts	
Almonds	Brazil nuts
Seeds	
All sprouted seeds	
Beans and Peas	
Limas	
Sugars	
Honey	
Vegetables	
All nonstarchy vegetables	

Nontraditional Vegetables	
Sea vegetables	Chlorophyll foods (wheatgrass, barley grass, alfalfa, spirulina, chlorella)
Herbs	

9. Why lemon and lime water?

In addition, drink one to two glasses of lime or lemon water (add 1 or 2 tablespoons of fresh lime or lemon juice to a glass of water) thirty minutes before each meal. Lime is actually more alkalinizing than lemons.

10. Enjoy chlorophyll foods and their benefit.

And finally, I recommend a high-chlorophyll drink such as Divine Health's Green Superfood.[16] High-chlorophyll foods will help to raise the urinary pH and buffer the acids.

11. Watch out for aluminum.

Avoid aluminum in any form since even small amounts can cause extensive bone loss. Aluminum is found in some antacids, aluminum cookware, aluminum cans, and aluminum coffeepots.

OSTEOPOROSIS, AMERICAN STYLE

While I was at a conference, a thirty-four-year-old woman asked me if I had any recommendations for osteoporosis other than the prescription medication Fosamax and 1,500 mg of calcium a day. This lady seemed much too young to be suffering with such a significant degree of osteoporosis. I questioned her, searching for a possible cause. Her mother didn't have osteoporosis. She appeared to be very healthy, and she had eaten a diet with adequate calcium and had exercised.

I continued to question her about her diet, and I learned that she had eaten the typical American diet I mentioned earlier in this chapter: She consumed soft drinks, a lot of meats, starches, salt, and sugar. In addition, she ate very few fruits and vegetables. She also drank too much coffee and tea.

Her typical American diet was actually destroying her bones. Her high-protein intake was leaching calcium out of her bones. The salty food she was consuming was robbing her bones as well. The high-sugar diet, together with the caffeine from the coffee, tea, and soft drinks, created an acidic environment in her body.

It cannot be repeated often enough: By eating the standard American diet, many individuals are doing just as this young woman did. They are creating such acidic conditions in their bodies that they are increasing their risk of developing osteoporosis, even at an early age.

Tips for Healthy Eating

In closing, let's review some important suggestions for preventing osteoporosis:

- Let half of your daily diet consist of fresh fruits and vegetables. This will create an alkaline environment in your body.

- Do not eat a lot of meats since they tend to form acid in the body.

- Foods that are high in oxalic acid include chocolate, spinach, rhubarb, cashews, asparagus, beet greens, and chard. These foods will inhibit the absorption of calcium; therefore, it is best to not take calcium supplements at the same time.

- Whole grains and fiber can also bind calcium. Therefore, it is best not to take calcium supplements at the same time as eating whole grains or fiber.

- Decrease intake of alcohol, coffee, tea, colas, and other caffeinated beverages since they create acidity that can leach calcium out of the bones.

- Avoid aluminum in any form.

- Decrease salt intake.

I strongly recommend my book *Eat This and Live!* for more information on a healthy diet.

GOD'S HELP

God will give you the wisdom, strength, and determination you need to plan a diet regime to build up your bones. Focus on the positive steps you can take to prevent osteoporosis, and take this valuable advice from God's Word:

> Don't be impressed with your own wisdom. Instead, fear the LORD and turn away from evil. Then you will have healing for your body and strength for your bones.

> —PROVERBS 3:7–8

A **BIBLE CURE** Prayer for You

Almighty God, give me the willpower to eat the foods that are best for me and to decrease or avoid those foods that rob my body of calcium. Help me to shop for the right calcium-rich foods to strengthen my bones and help prevent osteoporosis. Thank You for creating just the right foods for my body and for giving me the willpower to avoid junk foods and fad diets that will harm me. Amen.

A **BIBLE CURE** *Prescription*

List all the foods and beverages you now consume that
you need to avoid in the future.

_____

_____

_____

Now list the foods that you have been overlooking that you will begin
to include in your diet:

_____

_____

_____

Write a prayer asking God to guide you when you shop for the foods
you need to eat:

_____

_____

_____

_____

_____

_____

_____

_____

_____

3

CHARGE UP WITH EXERCISE

I F YOU HAVE osteoporosis, you may have suffered from painful fractures caused by weak and brittle bones. But I have good news for you. God cares very deeply about you! Everything about you is important to Him, even the strength of your bones. His powerful Word says, "I will search for my lost ones who strayed away, and I will bring them safely home again. I will bandage the injured and strengthen the weak" (Ezek. 34:16). God's desire and plan for you includes renewed health and strength.

Osteoporosis can steal the strength from your bones, leaving you stoop-shouldered and prone to fractures. But there is something you can do to help lower your risk for a break—you can exercise!

BENEFITING BONES WITH EXERCISE

Exercise can help prevent osteoporosis, and it can also help treat it by providing strength to your bones and muscles. Exercise will slow mineral loss, help you maintain good posture, and improve your overall fitness, which reduces the risk of falls.

Weight-bearing exercises and strengthening exercises are the most important forms of exercise in treating osteoporosis. However, using weights or calisthenics to build muscles will also help to build bones. Realize the stronger your muscles are, generally the stronger your bones are. For more information on this topic, please refer to my book *The Seven Pillars of Health*.

GET MOVING!

The sedentary lifestyle common in America is one of the greatest risks for eventually developing osteoporosis. Why? As I mentioned in chapter 1, the human bone is constantly being remodeled and reformed. But here's the key: this remodeling happens in response to the demands and stresses that are placed on the bone *by exercise*.

Weight-bearing exercises will actually stimulate the growth of new bone cells. The bones, however, must be stressed in order to grow. Weight-bearing exercise will not only stop bone loss but will also increase the mass of bone.

A sedentary lifestyle is eventually death to your bones. As a doctor, I have seen many women develop osteoporosis, and many of these women have had adequate amounts of calcium in their diets. But they don't stress their bones adequately through exercise, and, as a result, they lose significant amounts of bone.

> As soon as I pray, you answer me; you encourage me by giving me strength.
>
> —PSALM 138:3

Men also lose bone mass as they age, but not to the same degree as women. And is there any wonder this occurs? Most men and women are too tired to go to the gym when they get home from work, so they sit in their recliners and watch TV.

They limit their exercise to walking from the recliner to the kitchen and from the kitchen to the bedroom.

WEIGHT-BEARING EXERCISES

Which exercises will prevent osteoporosis? Many doctors encourage swimming and cycling, and these are wonderful exercises for improving your overall health. However, these exercises will not prevent osteoporosis. Only weight-bearing exercises will stimulate bone growth.[1] Cycling will stress the leg bones, but it will do nothing to stress the entire skeleton. Swimming puts no stress on the skeleton whatsoever and will not prevent osteoporosis.

Weight-bearing exercises such as dancing, walking, running, stair climbing, team sports, and yard work are often recommended in fighting osteoporosis. They are beneficial because they will stress (and thereby strengthen) the leg bones and hip bones. However, these activities are not as beneficial in preventing osteoporosis in the upper body—the spine, arms, and so forth.

The only exercises that prevent osteoporosis in the entire skeleton are weight-bearing exercises such as weightlifting and calisthenics. It's a well-known fact that, on average, weightlifters' bones are much thicker than those who don't lift weights. I highly encourage you to begin a weightlifting routine that will stress all of the major bones in your body and thus stimulate growth.

I am about to describe several simple weightlifting exercises that will benefit your bones. However, you may find it very helpful to join a gym and have a certified personal trainer demonstrate weightlifting exercises that will prevent osteoporosis.

A gym and trainer might be beyond your budget right now. If so, a "low-cost" option is to buy dumbbells and weightlifting sessions on DVD at a department store and begin a basic weight-lifting program right in your own home.

Perhaps you really don't think weightlifting is your thing, or you need a "no-cost" program. Don't worry! Performing calisthenics such as push-ups, lunges, squats, seated dips, or even lifting a five-pound bag of sugar, a can of paint, or a gallon of bottled water over your head will go a long way in improving your overall bone health.

GETTING STARTED

It's very important to know which exercises will benefit you and which ones you as an individual need to avoid. Never begin an exercise program—especially if you already have osteoporosis—without checking with your doctor first. Your doctor will help you tailor an exercise program to your specific needs.

If you've checked with your doctor, then you can begin doing some of these exercises right away. So, let's go!

Osteoporosis primarily affects the bones of the spine, hips, and forearms. Therefore, exercises tailored to prevent further loss to these three groups of bones are extremely important. Do these exercises approximately three times a week.

Overhead presses

While seated or standing, simply take a pair of 5- or 10-pound dumbbells and lift them over your head five to ten times. Repeat this for two to three sets.

Lunges

For beginners, start with your own body weight, and later you may add dumbells. To perform lunges, simply place the dumbbells down by your side and step forward with one foot and lunge outward. Then come back to a standing position with the feet together. Start with a comfortable number of repetitions, like three to five. Increase the number as you are comfortable, but eventually work up to eight to twelve repetitions for two or three sets if cleared by your physician or physical therapist.

Squats

Start with your own body weight with your hands behind your head, and go down and barely touch a chair or a short stool, depending on your height. Your buttocks should be parallel to the floor. If you cannot do this type of squat yet, then put a thick phone book, dictionary, or encyclopedia in the chair, and barely touch the book with your buttocks. Do not rest in the chair after each repetition. Eventually you should be able to perform eight to ten repetitions. As you get stronger, remove the books and eventually incorporate dumbells. Place the dumbbells by your side. (You can get larger, heavier dumbbells, such as 20- to 30-pound dumbbells that you hold with two hands.) With legs apart, simply squat down. These exercises are excellent for loading the hip joints, which will help prevent further bone loss. Start with a comfortable number of repetitions, like three to five. Increase the number as you are comfortable, but check with your physician or physical therapist for a recommended number of repetitions. I recommend eventually working up to eight to twelve repetitions for two to three sets.

Push-ups

Push-ups are great for preventing bone loss in the arms. However, many women cannot perform them. I recommend doing push-ups from the knees instead of from the feet. Performing these simple exercises will help you to prevent further bone loss and start building bone mass in the arms. Start with a comfortable number of repetitions like two or three. Increase the number as you are comfortable, but check with your physician or physical therapist for a recommended number of repetitions. I recommend eventually working up to eight to twelve repetitions for two to three sets.

I also recommend exercises to improve your posture. The chest stretch shown on the facing page, and several other exercises for improving your posture, can be found in my book *The Seven Pillars of Health*.

Chest Stretch 1: Extend arms across. Slightly squeeze shoulder blades backward, moving chest forward. Hold for ten seconds.

Chest Stretch 2: Align elbows with your shoulder at a ninety-degree angle against the frame of a wall or door. Move slightly forward so that your elbows are slightly behind you.

A FINAL WORD ABOUT WEIGHT CONTROL

If you have osteoporosis, maintaining your ideal weight can be an important factor. Remember, slenderness and leanness are risk factors for osteoporosis. So do not become too thin or too heavy, but maintain your ideal body weight. I strongly recommend my book *Dr. Colbert's "I Can Do This" Diet* if you have weight problems. Various national health organizations define an overweight adult as having a BMI between 25 and 29.9, while an obese adult is anyone who has a BMI of 30 or higher. They recommend maintaining a body mass index between 18.5 and

24.9 for optimum health. You can use the chart below to determine your own BMI by drawing a line from your weight (left column) to your height (right column). Is your BMI (middle column) in the healthy range?

A **BIBLE CURE** *Health Tip*

Body Mass Index Chart

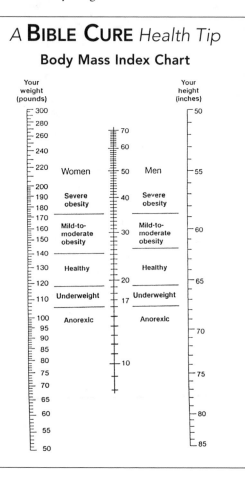

If you struggle with weight control, no one has to tell you how difficult maintaining your ideal weight can be. But don't despair—God's power can help. Ask Him to help you. He will. The Bible says, "Give all your worries and cares to God, for he cares about you" (1 Pet. 5:7). Give Him your discouragement, your hopelessness, your sense of defeat, and your lack of control. When you blow it, give it all back to Him again. You will be amazed at how much help you will receive. He is a great and wonderful heavenly Father, and nothing is too difficult for Him! (See Jeremiah 32:27.)

CHANGING THE FUTURE

Too many children now lead sedentary lifestyles due to the popularity of video and computer games that they play. When I was young, we played football, basketball, baseball, and other sports all year round. Today, most children simply play video games and watch TV, doing significantly less physical activity than their parents did years ago. We already have an epidemic of osteoporosis in our country, and most of these people with osteoporosis led fairly active lives in their youth. Think how much greater the epidemic of osteoporosis may be in the future when our children enter their fifties and sixties if they have lived sedentary lifestyles from childhood.

> My life is an example to many, because you have been my strength and protection. That is why I can never stop praising you; I declare your glory all day long. And now, in my old age, don't set me aside. Don't abandon me when my strength is failing.
>
> —PSALM 71:7–9

If you have children still at home, help them prevent osteoporosis by maintaining an active lifestyle that avoids destructive habits and foods. A person is never too young to begin to prepare his or her body for a long, prosperous life by following God's Bible Cure plan of exercise, nutrition, and positive attitudes.

A **BIBLE CURE** Prayer for You

Lord, deliver me from a sedentary lifestyle. Help me to keep my joints limber and my muscles well toned. Show me the level of exercise that is right for me at the present time. Give me the determination to get started, and help me maintain the discipline I need to keep going. Thank You for Your wisdom. Amen.

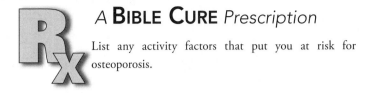

A **BIBLE CURE** *Prescription*

List any activity factors that put you at risk for osteoporosis.

_____

_____

List the exercises that you will be committed to doing every day to keep your posture straight and your bones and muscles strong.

_____

_____

Write a prayer to God casting your cares upon Him. End it with a word of thanks.

_____

_____

_____

_____

_____

_____

_____

_____

_____

4

BUILD UP WITH VITAMINS AND SUPPLEMENTS

T HE RECIPE FOR turning your health around may include a pound of effort mixed with a pinch of patience. The Word of God says, "Better to be patient than powerful; better to have self-control than to conquer a city" (Prov. 16:32).

Expecting to instantly reverse everything that has been happening in your body may be unrealistic. Remember, it has taken years and probably decades for your bones to degenerate. However, you can build up your body with wonderful supplements that provide the nutrients you need to battle and win over osteoporosis.

Eating correctly and taking supplements is a long-term process. Be persistent—not impatient. Don't get discouraged if you feel that you are not moving along quickly enough.

SIGNIFICANT SUPPLEMENTS

Start your journey toward feeling better by taking the significant supplements outlined in this chapter.

A good multivitamin

The foundation of a good supplement program always starts with a comprehensive multivitamin. Adequate doses of many of the nutrients I am about to discuss are found in a good multivitamin.

Calcium

This supplement's effectiveness can be reduced by whole grains containing phytic acid, which may reduce the absorption of calcium and other minerals. It is actually best to take calcium supplements after meals because hydrochloric acid in the stomach is increased with food and helps calcium absorption.

Stomach hydrochloric acid helps the absorption of calcium tremendously. The first part of the small intestines, called the duodenum, is the main place where it is absorbed. Remember, your body only absorbs about 20 to 30 percent of the calcium you consume.[1] The rest is excreted. Also, don't take all of your calcium at one time since your body can only absorb about 500 mg of calcium at one time.

This rate of calcium absorption can dip down as low as only 5 percent for calcium carbonate if you are a postmenopausal woman who is lacking hydrochloric acid. You could actually be taking in 1,500 mg of calcium carbonate a day and only absorbing 75 mg, which is only 5 percent. You can see by the loss of calcium daily through nonabsorption that taking 1,500 mg can still result in significant bone loss.

In addition, I do not recommend some sources of calcium. These include oyster shell since it may contain significant amounts of lead. Dolomite may also contain relatively high amounts of lead. So, be careful when buying calcium.

A chelated form of calcium, which is bound to an amino acid such as calcium citrate, calcium aspartate, or calcium fumarate, is more easily absorbed. Calcium hydroxyapatite, a form of calcium that is derived from bone, is absorbed fairly well. Because it comes from bone meal, it contains all the different minerals in their natural state. However, be careful not to purchase just any brand, for some can also contain lead. See the appendix for excellent calcium choices. Premenopausal women should take in 1,000 mg of chelated calcium or calcium hydroxyapatite a day, and postmenopausal women need 1,200 mg a day.

Calcium absorption is dependent upon vitamin D as well as bile, bile salts, and dietary fat. Patients with a low amount of stomach acid (a fairly common occurrence in postmenopausal women) need to take a well-absorbed calcium such as chelated calcium (see appendix) and not calcium carbonate. A chelated calcium does not need hydrochloric acid to be absorbed.

> He renews my strength. He guides me along right paths, bringing honor to his name. Even when I walk through the darkest valley, I will not be afraid, for you are close beside me. Your rod and your staff protect and comfort me.
>
> —PSALM 23:3–4

Vitamin D

As I mentioned in chapter 2, this is a fat-soluble vitamin found mainly in egg yolks, butter, salmon, mackerel, herring, and especially in fish-liver oils such as cod liver oil. Vitamin D is manufactured in our skin when it comes in contact with the sun's ultraviolet rays. Vitamin D not only is important in bone health but also helps with diabetes and inflammation and may protect you from heart disease, multiple sclerosis, autoimmune disease, cancer, and influenza. Since, as I mentioned earlier, it is difficult to get vitamin D from foods and most Americans are not exposed to adequate sunlight, I recommend vitamin D supplements. I typically recommend 2,000 IU (international units) per day of vitamin D for most patients, but I may increase the dose to 4,000 to 6,000 IU per day of vitamin D for a few months until the vitamin D level reaches the optimal range.

Even though cod liver oil is high in vitamin D, it also contains significant amounts of vitamin A. Studies have shown that high doses of vitamin A may increase your risk of a fracture. For example, some studies have shown that increased intake of vitamin A (retinol form) can increase your risk of a fracture by 40 percent.[2] For this reason, I do not recommend cod liver oil to patients with osteoporosis or osteopenia.

Strict vegetarians who do not eat any meat, eggs, or milk products and who do not get adequate sun exposure should take a multivitamin with at least 1,000 IU of vitamin D daily and perhaps 2,000 IU or higher, depending on their vitamin D_3 blood test.

Magnesium

This mineral helps to increase the absorption of calcium in your diet, and it also helps your bones to retain or hold on to the calcium. Without adequate amounts of magnesium you are more prone to losing bone more rapidly. The standard American diet provides inadequate amounts of magnesium. As I mentioned in chapter 2, caffeine, sugar, alcohol, and soft drinks cause magnesium to be depleted.

Magnesium is found naturally in dark green vegetables, nuts, seeds, and legumes, as well as whole grains such as whole wheat. Chlorophyll is the green pigment in plants, and the central atom of the chlorophyll is magnesium. Therefore, high-chlorophyll products are excellent sources of magnesium.

Because it can be hard to get enough magnesium from your diet, I recommend supplementing a balanced diet with a good comprehensive multivitamin, which will contain approximately 400 mg of magnesium. If you take calcium supplements, keep in mind that most calcium supplements do not contain magnesium, and calcium should be balanced with magnesium in approximately a two-to-one ratio.[3] In other words, if you consume 1,200 mg of calcium a day, you should take approximately 600 mg of magnesium a day.

There are certain types of coral calcium that are lead free and also contain both calcium and magnesium. (See appendix.)

> For I can do everything through Christ, who gives me strength.
> —Philippians 4:13

An acidic environment in the stomach is required for magnesium to be adequately absorbed. Eating a diet high in fats, proteins, or phosphorus may also hinder magnesium absorption. Similar to calcium, only about 40 percent of the magnesium that we consume is absorbed.[4] Chelated magnesium is the most absorbable form of magnesium, such as magnesium malate, magnesium asparate, or magnesium citrate. Magnesium salt, such as magnesium oxide and magnesium carbonate, is not nearly as easily absorbed as chelated varieties.

OTHER IMPORTANT NUTRIENTS FOR STRONG BONES

There are many nutrients that are very important for bone health and for reversing osteoporosis. In addition to calcium, magnesium, and vitamin D_3, which I have just discussed, additionally important are vitamin K_2, boron, vitamin B_6, vitamin B_{12}, folic acid, zinc, copper, vitamin C, potassium, phosphorus, manganese, silica, and strontium. Fortunately, most of these nutrients can be obtained in a good comprehensive multivitamin. Here is some additional information about many of these nutrients and their effect on bone health.

Vitamin K_2

It is interesting to note that as we age, our bones lose calcium and become brittle, but our arteries typically become calcified. However, vitamin K_2 is able to regulate calcium metabolism by keeping calcium in the bones and out of our arteries. Vitamin K is found in two different forms in nature: vitamin K_1, which is found in green leafy vegetables and is important in blood clotting, and the lesser-known vitamin K_2, which is found in egg yolks, organ meats, and dairy. Most physicians discourage patients from eating organ meats and eggs since they are both high in cholesterol, and, as a result, most Americans do not consume enough vitamin K_2.

However, in certain areas of Japan, a staple dish of fermented soybeans called "natto" is commonly eaten a few times a week and is very rich in vitamin K_2. The Japanese people who consume this dish typically have much higher blood levels of vitamin K_2 and significantly fewer occurrences of osteoporosis and bone fractures.[5] Vitamin K_2 has actually been cited as one of the most frequently prescribed treatments for osteoporosis in Japan.[6]

Vitamin K_2 causes an increase in the bone-building process and a decrease in the bone-loss process. If you take Coumadin, use of vitamin K_2 should be discussed with your doctor. For treating osteoporosis, I typically recommend at least 100 mcg (micrograms) per day of vitamin K_2, and many times I may recommend 1,000 mcg or more per day.

The B vitamin family

High levels of the toxic amino acid homocysteine are associated with fractures in patients with osteoporosis. It is very important to have your homocysteine level checked and to lower it to a level less than 10 micromoles per liter.[7]

Again, a good comprehensive multivitamin will contain B vitamins, folic acid, vitamin B_6, and vitamin B_{12} in doses that lower homocysteine levels. I recommend approximately 800 mcg per day of folic acid, approximately 500 mcg to 1,000 mcg per day of vitamin B_{12}, and approximately 10 mg to 20 mg per day of B_6.

Be sure to have your physician check your homocysteine level a few months after starting your multivitamin, and if it is still elevated a few months later, then I recommend adding 1,000 mg of trimethylglycine (also known as TMG) once or twice a day and 800 mcg of L5-methyltetrahydrofolate (L5MTHF) a day, which is an active form of folic acid.

Foods rich in vitamin B include green leafy vegetables, avocados, cantaloupe, almonds, and other nuts. Many doctors do not check homocysteine levels when diagnosing or treating osteoporosis, so be sure to ask your doctor about this very important lab test.

Boron

Boron is a mineral that is needed in trace amounts for healthy bones and is also necessary for the metabolism of calcium, phosphorus, and magnesium. A good comprehensive multivitamin will contain adequate amounts of boron, which is 2 mg to 3 mg a day.

Boron also helps to maximize the activity of estrogen and vitamin D in bone. Boron is involved in an enzyme reaction in the kidneys where vitamin D is converted to its most powerful bone-building form. Boron is also needed for the conversion of estrogen to its most powerful bone-building form, which is 17 beta-estradiol. Good food sources of boron are leafy green vegetables, legumes, nuts, apples, and pears.[8]

Strontium

Most people think of strontium as the toxic strontium 90, a toxic radioactive component of nuclear fallout and associated with increased risk of cancer. However, stable strontium is nonradioactive and nontoxic and is a trace mineral. It is also one of the most effective supplements found for the treatment of osteoporosis. Taking stable strontium can gradually eliminate radioactive strontium from the body. Strontium, found in seawater, is one of the most abundant trace minerals on earth. Strontium has also been used safely for more than one hundred years.[9]

One study involved 1,649 postmenopausal women with osteoporosis who received for three years either 680 mg of strontium a day or a placebo. The main bone mineral density of the lumbar spine increased in the strontium group by an average of 14.4 percent after three years. Strontium, when compared with the placebo, decreased the incidence of vertebral fractures by 49 percent after one year and by 41 percent after three years.[10]

Taking doses of strontium up to 1.7 g a day is a safe and effective way to treat osteoporosis. However, doses of 680 mg per day may be all that is needed to reverse osteoporosis. You can also boost your strontium intake by consuming the following foods: spices, seafood, whole grains, root and leafy vegetables, and legumes.[11]

Silicon

Silicon is also important for bone strength. It is found in high amounts in wheat, oat, and rice bran. It is also found in alfalfa and in the herb horsetail. Dark green vegetables, avocados, onions, and strawberries also contain silicon. This substance helps to restore and strengthen bones by strengthening the connective tissue collagen, which is at the matrix of the bone. Take the supplement as directed on the label. This is found in many comprehensive multivitamins.

MEDICATIONS FOR OSTEOPOROSIS

In the past, after menopause, women relied on hormone replacement therapy in order to keep their bones strong. However, recent studies have linked synthetic hormones with an increased risk of breast cancer and heart disease. Therefore, most doctors have abandoned hormone replacement therapy and are treating osteoporosis mainly with bisphosphonates.[12]

A **BIBLE CURE** *Health Fact*

Osteoporosis Is No Mystery!

It's no mystery why osteoporosis is so prevalent in this country. The average American woman only gets 450 mg of calcium a day—nowhere near the 1,000 to 1,200 mg that's needed to ward off the disease, says Susan Broy, MD, director of the Osteoporosis Center at the Advocate Medical Group in Chicago. Ironically, women—who need calcium even more than men do—are more likely to turn away from calcium-rich foods because they're more worried about their waistlines than their bones, Dr. Broy says.[13]

Getting enough calcium is especially important for women approaching menopause, when estrogen levels decline. Estrogen helps bones absorb and keep calcium. When estrogen levels fall, in many cases the bones become weaker. In fact, the highest rate of bone loss occurs in the first five to seven years after menopause. The sad thing about osteoporosis, says Dr. Broy, is that it's often preventable—if you get enough calcium.[14]

Bisphosphonates

These include Fosamax, Actonel, and Boniva. These medications are antiresorptive drugs that inhibit bone removal by osteoclast. These meds may reduce fracture rates by approximately 40 percent. However, these meds will also typically stay in your system for decades.[15]

Even though these medications do make your bones denser by preventing bone breakdown, they usually do not make your bones any stronger.[16] Realize that bone breakdown is a normal part of bone health, and without proper bone breakdown, new bones are not formed. So yes, you do get denser bones, but the bones may be more brittle.

This group of meds has also been linked to rare cases of osteonecrosis of the jawbone or jawbone decay.[17] This is a rare bone disease where the jawbone literally deteriorates and dies. Surgery is required to remove the dying jawbone, and many lose their teeth as a result.

These meds are also associated with inflammation of the esophagus and stomach ulcers in up to one-third of patients. They may also cause nausea, heartburn, constipation, diarrhea, abdominal pain, and musculoskeletal pain.

The bisphosphonate medications are better tolerated when taken in the once-a-month medication such as Boniva and Actonel.

Because of the side effects, I would only recommend bisphosphonates as a last resort or if you had severe osteoporosis. Realize in order to build strong bones, we need the necessary hormones, vitamins, minerals, protein, healthy diet, and exercise program.

Hormones

It is interesting to note in women after menopause that osteoporosis escalates mainly because the ovaries are no longer producing estrogen and progesterone, and testosterone levels are typically low. However, many doctors have abandoned hormone replacement therapy in women because of studies a few years ago, which show that women who take synthetic estrogens and progestins were at an increased risk of breast cancer, heart attacks, strokes, and pulmonary emboli. The patients were then taken off their synthetic hormones and not given the option of taking natural bioidentical hormones.[18] In other words, many in the medical community have unnecessarily dismissed *bioidentical* hormone replacement therapy as a viable option because of health risks women experienced with *synthetic* hormone replacement therapy.

I encourage you to talk to a doctor knowledgable in bioidentical hormone therapy. Unfortunately, most primary care physicians and gynecologists are uninformed. (See appendix for help in finding a doctor knowledgeable in bioidentical hormone therapy.) Then get a complete medical exam including a gynecological exam, breast exam, mammogram, Pap smear, and blood work, including hormone levels, before you start taking hormones. Hormone supplements should be added to your nutritional program only under the supervision of your doctor. Here are the hormones that are most helpful to your bone health:

Estrogen

We have known for decades that estrogen helps prevent and treat osteoporosis by slowing bone breakdown. Estrogen regulates the activity of osteoclasts, which break down bone. The estrogen actually curbs the activity of these bone-dissolving osteoclasts.

However, most doctors do not treat with bioidentical hormone creams. You will want to find a doctor who is knowledgeable in treating with bioidentical hormones and make sure the doctor is board certified. Also, be sure to get bioidentical estrogen in a liposomal transdermal cream and not in a pill because the pill increases the risk for weight gain and other side effects. (See appendix.)

Progesterone

While estrogen slows bone loss by curbing the activity of bone-dissolving *osteoclasts*, progesterone enables the bone-building *osteoblasts* to function properly. Simply put, progesterone stimulates new bone formation and is very important to bone health.

Progesterone is the first hormone that declines with age.[19] Women can have low progesterone levels as early as their twenties and thirties, which sets them up for bone loss and osteoporosis later on. Because of this, many women need to include progesterone in their hormone replacement therapy program.

Natural or bioidentical progesterone has a molecular structure identical to the progesterone that the ovaries naturally make. But unfortunately, most physicians still prescribe synthetic progesterone, which is actually progestin. This synthetic progesterone, or progestin, such as Provera, is not molecularly identical to the progesterone that your body makes and is known to have side effects including blood clots, fluid retention, weight gain, depression, and acne.

Again, you'll want to find a doctor who is knowledgeable in prescribing bioidentical progesterone. Your doctor may use either a liposomal transdermal cream or a capsule of progesterone at bedtime if you have insomnia issues. (See the appendix.)

Testosterone

Typically, men who develop osteoporosis have low testosterone levels. Osteoblasts depend on testosterone in order to help build new bone. Testosterone actually stimulates bone formation, helps to decrease calcium loss, and helps to maintain bone density.

Low doses of testosterone are also very effective in women who are fighting osteoporosis. I generally give either a transdermal testosterone cream or gel or a sublingual tablet in order to dissolve slowly in the mouth.

Realize that bioidentical estrogen, progesterone, and testosterone are all important in helping to build bone, and, again, you'll want to find a board-certified physician who is knowledgeable in prescribing testosterone in cream or gel form. (See the appendix.)

Parathyroid hormone (PTH)

This includes Forteo, which is recombinant human parathyroid hormone. It is used to treat osteoporosis by increasing both bone mass and bone strength. PTH stimulates new bone formation throughout the entire skeleton by stimulating osteoblastic activity. It also improves bone mineral density and increases bone strength. So in other words, you are getting denser and stronger bones and not denser brittle bones like the bisphosphonates.

Other medications

There are other medications used for osteoporosis, including selective estrogen receptor modulators such as Evista. However, these medications have side effects that increase the risk of stroke as well as uterine cancer. They also cause weight gain, hot flashes, and other side effects.[20]

The FDA has approved a medication called Reclast as a once-a-year treatment for osteoporosis. Reclast is administered through an IV, so it bypasses your digestive system as it goes to work to protect your bones from fracture for twelve months. Although I do believe a natural approach to bone health is best, I do recomment medications such as Reclast in severe cases of osteoporosis.

CONFUSION OVER CALCIUM SUPPLEMENTS

Before I close this chapter, I feel it is important to help clear up some confusion over calcium supplements. I have been asked the following questions many times since publishing the original edition of this book. Here are my answers:

Question: If I take calcium supplements, does that completely eliminate my risk of bone loss?

Answer: No! Many people—and even many physicians—are under the wrong impression that if you simply take a calcium supplement, you will not lose bone or develop osteoporosis. That is simply not true.

While calcium supplements are certainly a step in the right direction, the health of your bones depends on a number of different factors that affect your body's ability to absorb and utilize the calcium you consume. That's why it is important to implement all of the steps for healthy bones I have described for you in this book: proper diet, regular exercise, stress reduction, hormone therapy, and nutritional supplements.

Question: How do I know how much calcium I am getting from my supplements?

Answer: Let's start with an explanation of how to read the nutrition label of your supplement bottle and know exactly how much calcium your are consuming. First, don't be fooled by the milligrams of calcium in the calcium tablet. You want to find out the amount of *elemental calcium* instead, because that is the amount of calcium in each tablet that is actually available to be absorbed by your body. If the elemental calcium amount isn't clearly listed on the bottle, look for the amount listed in milligrams according to serving size on the Nutrition Facts label.

A **BIBLE CURE** *Health Tip*

Common Calcium Supplements[21]

Calcium Supplement	Strength of Tablet	Elemental Calcium Per Tablet
Calcium carbonate	650 mg	260 mg
	1,250 mg	500 mg
	1,500 mg	600 mg
Calcium citrate	950 mg	200 mg
Calcium gluconate	650 mg	58 mg
Calcium lactate	650 mg	84 mg
Calcium phosphate	500 mg	115 mg
	800 mg	304 mg

Question: What are the different types of calcium supplements, and are some better than others?

Answer: There are many forms of calcium, and this can lead to confusion. The two most common forms are calcium carbonate and calcium citrate. Other forms of calcium that have superior absorption compared with calcium carbonate and calcium citrate include calcium orotate, calcium aspartate, calcium malate, calcium citrate malate, and calcium formate. These amino acid chelated calciums are fairly expensive, and unfortunately, it is usually difficult to find most of these even in health-food stores. Calcium malate has a significantly better absorption rate than most other forms of calcium. (See appendix.) So let's talk about the two most commonly available forms of calcium supplements: calcium carbonate and calcium citrate.

Calcium carbonate

The most common calcium supplement on the market today is calcium carbonate, which is a calcium salt, and it is very inexpensive as well as very convenient. A 1,000-mg tablet of calcium carbonate contains 40 percent or 400 mg of elemental calcium, and it also contains 600 mg of the salt carbonate. So you are getting only 400 mg of elemental calcium in a 1,000-mg tablet.

Another issue to be aware of is that calcium carbonate may be very poorly absorbed on its own, but when taken with food, studies have shown that absorption of calcium carbonate is about the same as calcium citrate, approximately 30 percent.[22] For that reason, it is best to take calcium carbonate with food.

However, without food, significantly less calcium is absorbed. That means if you take 1,200 mg of calcium carbonate a day, which is a typical dose, it translates to only 480 mg of elemental calcium a day. At best, you only absorb around 30 percent of that amount with food. So instead of getting 1,200 mg a day, you are actually only getting 144 mg of calcium a day.

Calcium citrate

Calcium citrate is the other very common calcium supplement that is sold over the counter and is better absorbed than calcium carbonate. However, the calcium content is actually lower than calcium carbonate. Calcium citrate contains 21 percent elemental calcium.[23] So 1,000 mg of calcium citrate has only 210 mg of elemental calcium and 790 mg of citrate.

Some studies show that it has a better absorption than calcium carbonate, but when calcium carbonate is taken with food, the absorption is very similar: around 30 percent.[24] Therefore, 1,200 mg of calcium citrate has only 252 mg of elemental calcium. Since approximately 30 percent is absorbed, that means only about 75 mg of elemental calcium is actually absorbed.

Cal apatite (microcrystalline hydroxyapatite)

Another form of calcium worth mentioning is microcrystalline hydroxyapatite or MCHC. MCHC is a complex biological calcium salt and contains approximately forty minerals found naturally in bone in the proper ratio. It also contains collagen, amino acids, and glucosamine glycan. Hydroxyapatite is a combination of calcium and phosphorus bound in a special matrix structure in a two-to-one ratio. It is an excellent supplement to help stop bone loss and restore bone. See the appendix for more information.

Question: What about coral calcium?

Answer: Coral calcium has been advertised on TV for years. ConsumerLab.com, an independent testing lab, found that Coral Calcium Supreme had lead levels in excess of California standard for risk levels. There are similar lead dangers in oyster shell calcium, dolomite, and bone mill.

The calcium found in coral calcium is in the calcium carbonate classification. Coral calcium contains approximately seventy-four trace minerals and also contains magnesium not found in other calcium supplements. Feeding studies performed at the University of Ryukyu and Okinawa International University showed that absorption of calcium from coral calcium and experimental animals was actually better than the absorption of calcium from milk, hydroxyapatite, or calcium carbonate.[25] The majority of coral calcium comes from two suppliers who test every batch for lead and show proposition compliant lead levels. Coral calcium is actually obtained from fossilized coral reefs above sea level without disturbing the ecosystem. Below-sea coral calcium is highly contaminated due to industrial pollutants. Above-sea coral has not been subjected to the contaminants that the below-sea coral has. Also, coral calcium helps create an alkaline environment in the tissues.

Question: Are liquid calcium supplements or capsules better absorbed than tablets?

Answer: Many people have the idea that if calcium is dissolved in a liquid state, it is more easily absorbed. But this is not so, because the majority of liquid calcium supplements out there are calcium carbonate, which is poorly absorbed (remember, only about 10 percent when taken without food and only about 30 percent when taken with food is absorbed). However, one benefit of a liquid calcium supplement is that it may be easier for the elderly to swallow.

Calcium capsules usually dissolve better than calcium tablets. Some tablets are so tightly bound that they can take four to six hours to dissolve. Some of my patients have actually passed calcium tablets in their stools.

Calcium must dissolve in your stomach in order to be

absorbed by your intestines. USP supplements mean that the calcium is pure and contains no lead or other toxic metals. For more information on different types of calcium supplements, please refer to the appendix.

Obviously you can't absorb any nutrients from something that never even dissolved while passing through your body, so solubility is an important first step. However, you need to keep in mind that *solubility does not equal absorption.* It is not accurate to conclude that because a certain form of calcium is more easily *dissolved* by your body it is automatically more easily *absorbed.*

So remember, if you do take a calcium carbonate supplement, it is best absorbed with meals since the calcium absorption depends on adequate hydrochloric acid produced by the stomach. When taking calcium supplements, divide up the doses during the day. I recommend dividing the daily dose in three portions and taking one portion with each of your three daily meals since you can only absorb at most about 500 mg at a time.

Question: Do other foods, supplements, or medications affect my body's ability to absorb calcium?

Answer: Eating an orange, drinking lemon or lime water, or taking vitamin C supplements with calcium helps with the absorption of the calcium. Hydrochloric acid supplements also usually improve the absorption of calcium. But you should avoid taking iron supplements and calcium together. Also do not consume wheat bran or eat a big bowl of high-fiber cereal at the same time you take your calcium supplement because the phytic acid in the wheat bran will bind much of the calcium, as do foods high in oxalic acid such as spinach and chocolate.

Medications such as acid blockers, including Zantac, Pepcid, Prilosec, and Nexium, reduce the acid in your stomach that is required to absorb calcium carbonate. You then need a different form of calcium than we have discussed.

A **BIBLE CURE** *Health Tip*
Acid Blockers Increase Your Risk of Hip Fractures

A study led by Dr. Douglas Corley and published in the *Canadian Medical Association Journal* analyzed data on forty thousand patients taking acid-reducing drugs and found that people who took less than one pill a day had a 12 percent increase in fracture risk; people taking one pill a day had a 30 percent risk increase; those taking more than one pill a day experienced a 41 percent increase in their risk of fracture. The acid-reducing drugs reference in this study include Prevacid, Zantac, Nexium, Prilosec, Prontonix, and Aciphex.[26]

IT'S UP TO YOU

God has created all the substances you need to strengthen your bones and help you to prevent the onset of osteoporosis. Now your part is to use the vitamins and supplements your body needs to build stronger bones and resist disease.

Begin taking the steps you need to supplement your diet, especially with calcium. If you do it now, as you grow older you will enjoy a more active, vital life serving God and celebrating the abundance of good things that He has planned for you.

Jesus said, "My purpose is to give them a rich and satisfying life" (John 10:10). His abundance isn't just for you in your youth, but as you grow older as well.

> But those who trust in the LORD will find new strength. They will soar high on wings like eagles. They will run and not grow weary. They will walk and not faint.
>
> —ISAIAH 40:31

God plans for the autumn and winter of your life to be fruitful, that is, full of activity, excitement, and strength. His powerful Word says, "But the godly will flourish like palm trees and grow strong like the cedars of Lebanon. For they are transplanted to the LORD's own house. They flourish in the courts of our God. Even in old age they will still produce fruit; they will remain vital and green" (Ps. 92:12–14).

A **BIBLE CURE** Prayer for You

Creator God, thank You for giving wisdom to men to discover and understand the supplements and vitamins I need to help my body prevent and overcome osteoporosis. I thank You that You desire for me to have health and an abundant, full life throughout all of my mature years. Grant me the wisdom to discover what my body needs to grow old both in grace and health. Amen.

A **BIBLE CURE** *Prescription*

Check the supplements you need to start using to strengthen your bones:

❏ Calcium

❏ Magnesium

❏ Vitamin D

❏ A multivitamin, including B_6, B_{12}, folic acid, boron, and silicon

❏ Vitamin K_2

❏ Strontium

❏ Natural progesterone cream

Memorize this encouraging Bible Cure text:

> I love you, LORD; you are my strength. The LORD is my rock, my fortress, and my savior; my God is my rock, in whom I find protection. He is my shield, the power that saves me, and my place of safety.
>
> —PSALM 18:1–2

5

LOOK UP WITH DYNAMIC FAITH

AVE YOU BEEN told that you have osteoporosis? Believe God for a miracle. He can give you a miracle healing. I've witnessed such miracles many times, and I have experienced the miracle-working power of God in my own body. But if miracles happened every time we wanted them to happen, they wouldn't be miracles anymore—they would be cures!

Miracles are a divine touch, a moment of supernatural intervention when total healing occurs—but all healing is from God. A doctor can sew up an incision and bind up a wound. But the power that heals the wound and makes you well again always comes from God. I encourage you to pray for a miracle, but don't stop there. Lay hold of the principles of health outlined in this book to aid the healing process. I have found over the years that God generally won't do what you can do. In addition, let's look at osteoporosis in another way that you may not have thought of.

ANOTHER DIMENSION

Throughout this book we have taken a close look at the physical side of osteoporosis. But another dimension exists to this disease that we must also address: a spiritual and emotional dimension.

The Bible strongly suggests that bone disease sometimes has an emotional and spiritual component. Do you know that negative emotions can affect your bones? According to the Bible, they can.

CHEER UP

Proverbs 17:22 says, "A merry heart does good, like medicine, but a broken spirit dries the bones" (NKJV). A broken spirit is a spirit that's dejected, and this hurting, depressed spirit will eventually lead to physical and emotional fatigue and a lack of desire to exercise and remain active. Eventually, osteoporosis can result.

> A merry heart does good, like medicine, but a broken spirit dries the bones.
> —PROVERBS 17:22, NKJV

God didn't create you to be sad. If you've experienced problems and situations that have robbed you of your joy, turn those circumstances over to God. You'll be amazed at how much He really does love you and how able He is to help you if you let Him. Can you imagine a parent who would want his or her child to be sad instead of happy? Of course not. God is your heavenly Father, and He desires for you to have joy. Why don't you let Him give you His own peace and joy by surrendering your sorrow to Him?

Sadness is only one negative emotion that can affect your bones. Let's look at another.

PERSECUTION STRIKES TO THE BONE

Have you ever felt persecuted? Perhaps a family member just simply dislikes you. Perhaps someone you thought was a friend has gossiped about you. Perhaps a co-worker takes all of the credit for your accomplishments and gives you the blame for his or her failures. Whatever the source, persecution didn't end with the saints of the first-century church. There's plenty of it around today. And, believe it or not, the Bible suggests that persecution can also affect your bones.

The psalmist says, "Have mercy on me, O LORD, for I am weak; O LORD, heal me, for my bones are troubled....My eye wastes away because of grief; it grows old because of all my enemies" (Ps. 6:2, 7, NKJV). When David wrote this psalm, he was experiencing so much persecution that his bones were affected.

Psalm 42:9–10 says something similar: "'Why do I go mourning because of the oppression of the enemy?' As with a breaking of my bones, my enemies reproach me, while they say to me all day long, 'Where is your God?'" (NKJV).

Although we no longer commonly use words like *persecution* and *affliction*, injustices and personal assaults feel the same to an individual regardless of the generation into which he was born.

We may grin and bear them, but personal attacks, assaults, and various forms of injustice strike deeply into our hearts and affect our bodies. The Bible says that when these attacks come often, our bones can be impacted.

God's Word suggests that our physical well-being and emotional well-being are linked together. Environmental stress can take a toll as well. Anxiety, depression, and long-term stress all raise the cortisol level in our bodies. Elevated cortisol over a long period of time leads to bone loss and may evenually lead to osteoporosis, similar to cortisone medications such as prednisone.

LESS STRESS

One significant factor that will rob your body of calcium and make you vulnerable to osteoporosis is stress. Calcium absorption may also be decreased by emotional and physical stress.

God's plan is for you to handle stress by casting your cares on Him. "Give all your worries and cares to God, for he cares about you" (1 Pet. 5:7).

What cares have you neglected to give to God?

- Financial concerns
- Hurting relationships
- Future goals
- Job-related anxieties
- Other: _____

God cares for you and wants to see you through all the stress and worry you may be facing. If you hold on to your stress, then your body will suffer, including your bones! Surrender your cares to Him.

Stress can impact you the same as having a troubled soul.

A TROUBLED SOUL

There is another negative emotion that can lead to bone disease. It is a troubled heart or soul. Have you ever felt deeply troubled? Perhaps it was over something you did or something you witnessed. Hiding such things deep inside can eat away at you and eventually impact your bones. The Bible says, "When I kept silence, my bones waxed old through my roaring all the day long" (Ps. 32:3, KJV).

Such troubling of a person's heart can be caused by a sense of guilt. Make no mistake; guilt is a powerful emotion! Every individual is different. One person may be deeply troubled by something another would scarcely think about twice. That doesn't matter. What does matter is that we keep our hearts clean before God.

> Blessed is he whose transgression is forgiven, whose sin is covered. Blessed is the man unto whom the LORD imputeth not iniquity, and in whose spirit there is no guile.
>
> —PSALM 32:1–2

If you have trouble in your soul, kneel down and pray in private. Confess all that is troubling you to God. The cleansing you will receive will feel like a breath of fresh, clean air to your soul. None of us were made to carry the weight of guilt around. Jesus Christ died on the cross to rid your life of guilt and sadness forever. He paid the price of sin so that you wouldn't have to. He made a way so that you might live unencumbered and free. He made it so simple.

You can find the answer to every negative emotion in Him.

The best stress relievers are contentment, gratitude, joy, and laughter. Christians should be the happiest people on earth. We are to be the light of the world and the salt of the earth. We are Christ's ambassadors on the earth.

Did you know that children laugh about four hundred times a day, but adults only laugh about ten to fifteen times? We need more laughter in our lives. As I mentioned earlier, Proverbs 17:22 says, "A merry heart does good, like medicine" (NKJV). In many of my books, I prescribe ten belly laughs a day. But before you can enjoy a really good laugh, you have to identify what I call "joy stealers" in your life.

JOY STEALERS

There are three main types of joy stealers I commonly see in my practice.

Drainers

Realize that some people don't want to be happy, especially depressed people. These people are negative and drain your energy. The less time you spend with these depletors, the better off you are. Philippians 2:14 says, "Do all things without grumbling, fault-finding, or complaining."

Irritators

Some people learn to push your buttons and purposely irritate, frustrate, and manipulate you. They hold the Xbox controller and are pushing your buttons manipulating you. Make a decision to refuse to let them control you, and simply overlook it and let it go.

Changers

Many couples are not happy because they are trying to change each other. They think, "I will be happy when my spouse changes." Instead of trying to change each other, just relax and let God change you.

Circumstances

Too many people are waiting for their circumstances to get worked out before they decide to be happy. They say or think things like: "As soon as I get a better job I will be happy." "As soon as I am out of debt I will be happy."

Joy is a decision and a choice that you make in spite of circumstances. Joy must become a habit. It starts with learning to be content.

Contentment

In Philippians 4:11, Paul said, "I have learned to be content with whatever I have." Contentment did not happen automatically. Paul had to train his mind to stay content. It starts with practicing gratitude. One of the best ways to practice gratitude is to keep a gratitude journal and read it aloud each day. Simply make a list of all the things in your life that you can be thankful for. Quit focusing on what you don't have, and start thanking God for what you do have. Put on the garment of praise for the spirit of heaviness (Isa. 61:3).

I speak about gratitude in many of my books because the power of practicing gratitude in your life has many effects on your health. Gratitude unsticks the stress response and helps you break the power of negative emotions in your life. For more information on the benefits of gratitude, refer to my book *Stress Less.*

BREAKING THE POWER OF NEGATIVE EMOTIONS

You can eliminate negative thoughts and emotions by spiritually feeding on God's Word. Here are some places you can turn to break the power of negative thoughts and emotions in your life:

- Overcoming anger (Eph. 4:26–27)
- Overcoming bitterness (Eph. 4:31–32)
- Overcoming anxiety (Phil. 4:6–7)
- Overcoming fear (2 Tim. 1:7)
- Overcoming guilt (1 John 1:9)

Proverbs 14:30 says, "A sound heart is the life of the flesh: but envy the rottenness of the bones" (KJV). However, Proverbs 16:24 says, "Pleasant words are as an honeycomb, sweet to the soul, and health to the bones" (KJV).

You see, a broken spirit, shame, and envy can destroy the bones, but pleasant, healing words can build them. If you have osteoporosis, or if you have osteopenia, read the Bible and speak the Word of God aloud. God's Word is full of power and truth. It can change your heart and redirect your emotions.

ACCENT THE POSITIVE!

As you begin to follow the Bible Cure for osteoporosis, you also need to cultivate a positive attitude based on the fruit of God's Spirit so that you can overcome any worry or anxiety that may be paralyzing your efforts. In Galatians 5:22–23 we read, "But the Holy Spirit produces this kind of fruit in our lives: love, joy, peace, patience, kindness, goodness, faithfulness, gentleness, and self-control. There is no law against these things!" Make the decision now to let these attitudes direct your decisions to win the battle against osteoporosis.

Take These Bible Cure Steps

Let me suggest that you initiate these spiritual steps to undergird everything you do in the natural to defeat osteoporosis:

1. Resist worry.

Becoming anxious about your future will only serve to weaken you physically and spiritually. Worry never overcame anything. The Bible promises:

> Always be full of joy in the Lord. I say it again—rejoice!...Don't worry about anything; instead, pray about everything. Tell God what you need, and thank him for all he has done. Then you will experience God's peace, which exceeds anything we can understand. His peace will guard your hearts and minds as you live in Christ Jesus.
>
> —Philippians 4:4, 6–7

Replace worry with the confidence and the peace that God's plan for you will overcome osteoporosis.

2. Pray.

Prayer is an unlimited resource for filling your life with God's Spirit, wisdom, and strength. He will strengthen your skeletal system and give you the determination to take the natural steps you need to walk in health. Take to heart these encouraging words from the Book of Psalms:

> I love the LORD because he hears my voice and my prayer for mercy. Because he bends down to listen, I will pray as long as I have breath! Death wrapped its ropes around me; the terrors of the grave overtook me. I saw only trouble and sorrow. Then I called on the name of the LORD: "Please, LORD, save me!" How kind the LORD is! How good he is! So merciful, this God of ours! The LORD protects those of childlike faith; I was facing death, and he saved me. Let my soul be at rest again, for the LORD has been good to me. He has saved me from death, my eyes from tears, my feet from stumbling. And so I walk in the LORD's presence as I live here on earth!
>
> —PSALM 116:1–9

3. Trust in God's Word to heal and sustain you.

Throughout this book are scriptures that will strengthen and encourage you. Learn them. Speak them aloud. Let His Word bring guidance and healing into your life.

> "Lord, help!" they cried in their trouble, and he saved them from their distress. He sent out his word and healed them, snatching them from the door of death. Let them praise the Lord for his great love and for the wonderful things he has done for them.
>
> —PSALM 107:19–21

4. Start smiling.

Joy is demonstrated to others by smiling. A smile sends a message to the whole body that you are happy. When you smile, powerful endorphins and neurotransmitters are released in your body. This results in an elevated mood.

Don't wait for your problems to go away before you start smiling; smile now and watch God begin to turn your problems around.

5. Start laughing.

There are many health benefits of laughter, which is why, as I mentioned earlier, I recommend ten belly laughs a day. Among other things, laughter releases stress and tension and stimulates the relaxation response in your body, enabling you to relax. Laughter improves sleep, relieves pain, and improves brain function. It also reduces your risk of heart attack and improves your immune system.

A **BIBLE CURE** Prayer for You

Heavenly Father, help me to apply all of these things I have learned. I take Your hand for the rest of my journey through the seasons of my life. Help me to walk in divine health throughout the path You lay before me and to know You better all along the way. Lord, help me to speak and think positive words so that my life will bring help and refreshing to others. Give me the power to stop destructive habits and attitudes. Fill me with Your joy for life, and give me energy to take the necessary steps to stay fit, both physically and spiritually all of my days. Amen.

A **BIBLE CURE** *Prescription*

What do you need to overcome in your attitude and outlook on life?

- Bitterness
- Negative thoughts
- Anxiety
- Sadness
- Excessive worry and stress
- Speaking destructive instead of encouraging words
- Other: _____

Check the spiritual steps you have started in overcoming osteoporosis:

- ❏ I have stopped worrying.
- ❏ I am praying.
- ❏ I am learning and applying God's Word.
- ❏ I am trusting God for health and strength.

Write a prayer thanking God for all the ways He has created to help you overcome osteoporosis in your life:

_____

_____

_____

_____

_____

BEGIN A BRAND-NEW LIFE—TODAY!

AFTER READING THIS book, you now have an understanding that as we age, we gradually lose more and more bone. But there is hope for slowing, stopping, and even reversing bone loss. In this book, I have recommended the following steps to you:

- Change your diet, and limit the intake of animal protein and sugar and highly processed carbohydrates.

- Limit your alcohol as well as caffeine intake.

- Eat more alkaline foods such as vegetables and fruits, and refer to the list of alkaline foods in my book *The Seven Pillars of Health*, pages 170–171.

- Begin consuming foods that are higher in calcium. See my recommendations in *Eat This and Live!* pages 92–93.

- Have your hormone levels checked, including estradiol, progesterone, and testosterone. Make an appointment with a doctor who is knowledgeable in prescribing bioidentical hormones.

- Begin a regular exercise program consisting of weight-bearing exercises, such as walking, as well as resistance training.

- Realize that most American diets are low in certain nutrients that are critically important for building bones. Therefore, include in your supplement program a comprehensive multivitamin as well as a supplement including vitamin D_3, vitamin K_2, magnesium, and perhaps strontium.

- Finally, remember that chronic stress, anxiety, and depression will cannibalize your bones. However, a merry heart is better than any medicine since it has no side effects. Learn to cope with stress, and an important way in coping with stress is including ten belly laughs a day.

God cares about you today, and He cares about your tomorrows. He can see the path that stretches out ahead of you beyond your view. With faith, wisdom, healthy habits, and God's wonderful love, I trust He will take you from whatever season of life you are experiencing right now all the way through the winter of your life with health, vitality, energy, and strength.

I encourage you to make a bold commitment to a healthy tomorrow by beginning to implement the Bible Cure plan outlined in this book today. Remember, God has provided all that you need for health and healing. He is all you need, so never stop looking to Him.

—DON COLBERT, MD

A PERSONAL NOTE
From Don Colbert

GOD DESIRES TO heal you of disease. His Word is full of promises that confirm His love for you and His desire to give you His abundant life. His desire includes more than physical health for you; He wants to make you whole in your mind and spirit as well as through a personal relationship with His Son, Jesus Christ.

If you haven't met my best friend, Jesus, I would like to take this opportunity to introduce Him to you. It is very simple. If you are ready to let Him come into your life and become your best friend, all you need to do is sincerely pray this prayer:

> *Lord Jesus, I want to know You as my Savior and Lord. I believe You are the Son of God and that You died for my sins. I also believe You were raised from the dead and now sit at the right hand of the Father praying for me. I ask You to forgive me for my sins and change my heart so that I can be Your child and live with You eternally. Thank You for Your peace. Help me to walk with You so that I can begin to know You as my best friend and my Lord. Amen.*

If you have prayed this prayer, you have just made the most important decision of your life. I rejoice with you in your decision and your new relationship with Jesus. Please contact my publisher at pray4me@strang.com so that we can send you some materials that will help you become established in your relationship with the Lord. We look forward to hearing from you.

NUTRITIONAL SUPPLEMENTS FOR OSTEOPOROSIS

Divine Health nutritional products

1908 Boothe Circle
Longwood, FL 32750
Phone: (407) 331-7007
Web site: www.drcolbert.com
E-mail: info@drcolbert.com

Bone support: Divine Health Cal-Mag-D3, calcium malate, chelated calcium, Divine Health Chelated Magnesium, coral complex (coral calcium), folic acid, Divine Health Natural Progesterone Cream, Pro Bono (a comprehensive bone support formula containing all major bone building nutrients), Divine Health Strontium, Divine Health Vitamin D3, and Divine Health Vitamin K2

Comprehensive multivitamin: Divine Health Multivitamin and Divine Health Living Multivitamin

Hormone health: Divine Health Natural Progesterone Cream

Omega oils: Divine Health Omega Pure and Divine Health Living Omega

Chlorophyll foods: Green Superfood, Living Food

Metagenics

Cal Apatite (microcrystalline hydroxyapatite) with Boron
Phone: (800) 692-9400 (refer to #W7741 when ordering)
Web site: www.drcolbert.meta-ehealth.com

OsteoSun by Cell Tech

For coenzyme Q_{10} to be taken with red yeast ricec
Phone: (800) 939-3909

WorldHealth.net

A global resource for antiaging medicine and to find a doctor that specializes in bioidentical hormone therapy

NOTES

CHAPTER 1—WISE UP TO WIN

1. Carolyn Riester O'Connor and Sharon Perkins, *Osteoporosis for Dummies* (Indianapolis, IN: Wiley Publishing, Inc., 2005), 51.

2. National Institute of Arthritis and Musculoskeletal and Skin Disorders, "Osteoporosis," http://www.niams.nih.gov/Health_Info/Bone/Osteoporosis/default.asp (accessed June 30, 2009).

3. Ibid.

4. Ibid.

5. National Institute of Arthritis and Musculoskeletal and Skin Disorders, "Information About the Musculoskeletal and Skin Systems," http://science.education.nih.gov/supplements/nih6/Bone/guide/info_musculo_skin-a.htm (accessed July 6, 2009).

6. "Best Calcium Supplements," Herbal-Supplements-Guide.com, http://www.herbal-supplements-guide.com/best-calcium-supplements.html (accessed July 6, 2009).

7. O'Connor and Perkins, *Osteoporosis for Dummies*, 24.

8. Tori Hudson, *Women's Encyclopedia of Natural Medicine* (New York: McGraw Hill Companies, 2008), 238.

9. William S. Pietrzak, *Musculoskeletal Tissue Regeneration* (New York: Humana Press, 2008), 48. Accessed on Google Books on July 6, 2009.

10. Hudson, *Women's Encyclopedia of Natural Medicine*.

11. Pietrzak, *Musculoskeletal Tissue Regeneration*.

12. "Osteoporosis Home Test," HealthyNewAge.com, http://www
    .healthynewage.com/osteoporosis-progesterone.htm (accessed
    July 6, 2009).

13. John N. Fordham, *Osteoporosis: Your Questions Answered*
    (Philadelphia, PA: Elsevier Health Sciences, 2004), 18.
    Accessed on Google Books on July 6, 2009.

14. Jack Challem, *User's Guide to Nutritional Supplements* (Laguna
    Beach, CA: Basic Health Publications, Inc., 2003) 107.
    Accessed on Google Books on July 6, 2009.

15. "With So Many Uses for Calcium, What Is the Best Way to
    Take It?" NoumenaNaturopathic.com, http://www.noumena
    .ca/advice/calcium.php (accessed July 6, 2009).

16. Ibid., 56.

17. Brigham and Women's Hospital, "Hip Fracture," http://
    healthlibrary.brighamandwomens.org/Library/Encyclopedia/
    85,P08957 (accessed June 30, 2009).

18. O'Connor and Perkins, *Osteoporosis for Dummies*, 134–135.

19. "Osteoporosis," University of Medicine and Dentistry of New
    Jersey, http://www.healthynj.org/dis-con/osteo/main.htm
    (accessed July 6, 2009).

20. "Osteoporosis: A New Era in Recognition and Treatment,"
    MedScape.com, http://cme.medscape.com/viewarticle/461563
    (accessed July 6, 2009).

CHAPTER 2—POWER UP WITH NUTRITION

1. National Institutes of Health, "Calcium From Other Foods," http://www.nichd.nih.gov/milk/prob/other_foods.cfm (accessed June 30, 2009).

2. U.S. Department of Health and Human Services, U.S. Department of Agriculture, "Dietary Guidelines for Americans 2005," Health.gov, http://www.health.gov/dietaryguidelines/dga2005/document/pdf/DGA2005.pdf (accessed July 6, 2009).

3. Susan Lang, "Eating Less Meat May Help Reduce Osteoporosis Risk, Studies Show," *Cornell Chronicle*, http://www.news.cornell.edu/chronicle/96/11.14.96/osteoporosis.html (accessed July 6, 2009).

4. Harris H. McIlwain and Debra Fulghum Bruce, "Super Nutrients That Keep Bones Strong," FamilyResource.com, http://www.familyresource.com/health/nutrition-for-adults/super-nutrients-that-keep-bones-strong (accessed July 6, 2009).

5. Brandon Johnsonn, "Foods High in Magnesium," EnzineArticles.com, http://ezinearticles.com/?Foods-High-in-Magnesium&id=877522 (accessed July 6, 2009).

6. John Jacob Cannell, "Up to 70 Percent of Americans May be Deficient in Vitamin D," http://74.125.95.132/search?q=cache:13pTlqVa74UJ:www.absolute.bz/images/Up_to_70_Percent_of_Americans_May_be_Deficient_in_Vitamin_D.doc+70+percent+of+the+U.S.+population+has+vitamin+D3+levels+below+35+mg/mL&cd=1&hl=en&ct=clnk&gl=us (accessed June 30, 2009).

7. Medline Plus, "25-hydroxy Vitamin D Test," http://
   medlineplus.nlm.nih.gov/medlineplus/ency/article/003569
   .htm (accessed June 30, 2009).

8. "Red Yeast Rice Promotes Bone Formation,"
   ChineseMedicineNews.com, June 7, 2008, http://chinese
   medicinenews.com/2008/06/07/red-yeast-rice-promotes-bone
   -formation/ (accessed July 1, 2009).

9. Ibid.

10. Susan E. Brown, "The Importance of pH Balance in Healthy
    Bones," BetterBones.com, May 19, 2009, http://www
    .betterbones.com/alkalinebalance/default.aspx (accessed July 1,
    2009).

11. Charles E. Ophardt, "pH Scale," Virtual Chembook: Elmhurst
    College, http://www.elmhurst.edu/~chm/vchembook/184ph
    .html (accessed July 1, 2009).

12. Ben Kim, "Essential Details on Acid and Alkaline-Forming
    Effects of Food and How Your Body Maintains a Healthy
    pH," DrBenKim.com, July 28, 2008, http://www.drbenkim
    .com/ph-body-blood-foods-acid-alkaline.htm (accessed July 1,
    2009).

13. Arthur C. Guyton, *Textbook of Medical Physiology*, 8th ed.
    (Philadelphia, PA: Saunders Co. Ltd., 1990), 331, 340, 711, as
    viewed at http://www.enotes.com/science-fact-finder/human
    -body/what-normal-ph-blood-urine-saliva (accessed July 1,
    2009).

14. "Screening Your Urine and Saliva pH to Identify an Acid
    System," TargetYourHealth.org, http://www.targetyourhealth
    .org/reference/acid.htm (accessed July 1, 2009).

15. "Neutralizing Acidosis and Bone Loss Among Mature Adults," ScienceDaily.com, February 11, 2009, http://www.sciencedaily .com/releases/2009/01/090131124439.htm (accessed July 1, 2009).

16. Donald Colbert, *Dr. Colbert's Guide to Ultimate Health* (Orlando, FL: Benny Hinn Ministries, 1999), 48.

Chapter 3—Charge Up With Exercise

1. Melinda Thompson, "Weight Bearing Exercises," Suite101.com, http://womenshealth.suite101.com/article.cfm/weight_bearing_ exercises (accessed July 6, 2009).

Chapter 4—Build Up With Vitamins and Supplements

1. Challem, *User's Guide to Nutritional Supplements*, 107.

2. PubMed, "Vitamin A Intake and Hip Fractures Among Postmenopausal Women," http://www.ncbi.nlm.nih.gov/ pubmed/11754708 (accessed June 30, 2009).

3. "How to Best Absorb Calcium Supplements," eHow.com, http://www.ehow.com/how_3953_absorb-calcium-supplements .html (accessed July 6, 2009).

4. "Magnesium in Depth," BodyAndFitness.com, http://www .bodyandfitness.com/Information/Health/Research/magnesium .htm (accessed July 6, 2009).

5. M. Kaneki, S. J. Hodges, T. Hosoi, et al., "Japanese Fermented Soybean Food as the Major Determinant of the Large Geographic Difference in Circulating Levels of Vitamin K2: Possible Implications for Hip-fracture Risk," *Nutrition* 17, no. 4 (2001): 315–321, as quoted in William Davis, "Protecting Bone and Arterial Health With Vitamin K2," *Life Extension* magazine, March 2008, as viewed online at http://www.lef.org/magazine/mag2008/mar2008_Protecting-Bone-And-Arterial-Health-With-Vitamin-K2_01.htm (accessed July 1, 2009).

6. Steven M. Plaza and Davis W. Lamson, "Vitamin K2 in Bone Metabolism and Osteoporosis," *Alternative Medicine Review* 10, no. 1 (2005): 24–35, as viewed online at http://findarticles.com/p/articles/mi_m0FDN/is_1_10/ai_n13557316/ (accessed July 1, 2009).

7. "Homocysteine Testing," GetHSmart.com, http://www.gethsmart.com/testing.html (accessed July 1, 2009).

8. Joseph Pizzorno, "Strong Bones for Life—Naturally (Part 2)," WebMD blog, October 16, 2008, http://blogs.webmd.com/integrative-medicine-wellness/2008/10/strong-bones-for-life-naturally-part-2.html (accessed July 1, 2009).

9. Ward Dean, "Strontium: Breakthrough Against Osteoporosis," American Academy of Anti-Aging Medicine, May 5, 2004, http://www.worldhealth.net/news/strontium_breakthrough_against_osteoporo (accessed July 1, 2009).

10. P. J. Meunier, C. Roux, E. Seeman, et al., "The Effects of Strontium Ranelate on the Risk of Vertebral Fracture in Women With Postmenopausal Osteoporosis," *New England Journal of Medicine* 350, no. 5 (January 2004): 459–468, as viewed at http://content.nejm.org/cgi/content/abstract/350/5/459 (accessed July 1, 2009).

11. Dean, "Strontium: Breakthrough Against Osteoporosis," http://www.worldhealth.net/news/strontium_breakthrough_against_osteoporo (accessed July 1, 2009).

12. National Cancer Institute, "Menopausal Hormone Replacement Therapy (HRT)," October 3, 2006, http://www.cancernet.gov/clinicaltrials/digest-postmenopausal-hormone-use (accessed July 6, 2009).

13. Selene Yeager, *New Foods for Healing* (New York: Rodale Press, 1999), 396.

14. Ibid.

15. Ethel S. Siris, Steven T. Harris, Clifford J. Rosen, et al., "Adherence to Bisphosphonate Therapy and Fracture Rates in Osteoporotic Women: Relationship to Vertebral and Nonvertebral Fractures From 2 US Claims Databases," Mayo Clinic Proceedings, http://www.mayoclinicproceedings.com/content/81/8/1013.full (accessed July 6, 2009).

16. Phuli Cohan, "Bone Density Drugs Can Kill Your Bones—Canadian Study Confirms," http://phulicohanmd.com/?m=200803 (accessed July 6, 2009).

17. John T. Grbic, Regina Landesberg, Shou-Qing Lin, et al., "Incidence of Osteonecrosis of the Jaw in Women With Postmenopausal Osteoporosis," *Journal of the American Dental Association* 139, no. 1, 2008: 32–40, as viewed online at http://jada.ada.org/cgi/content/full/139/1/32 (accessed July 6, 2009).

18. J. E. Rossouw, G. L. Anderson, R. L. Prentice, et al., "Risks and Benefits of Estrogen Plus Progestin in Healthy Postmenopausal Women: Principal Results From the Women's Health Initiative Randomized Controlled Trial," *Journal of the American Medical Association* 288, no. 3, (July 2002): 321–333, as quoted in David Tuttle, "Pioneer of Natural Female Hormone Replacement," *Life Extension* magazine, April 2005, http://www.lef.org/magazine/mag2005/apr2005_report_female_02.htm (accessed July 6, 2009).

19. Tuttle, "Pioneer of Natural Female Hormone Replacement."

20. "Side Effects," Evista.com, http://www.evista.com/pat/pat330_side_effects.jsp (accessed July 6, 2009).

21. O'Connor and Perkins, *Osteoporosis for Dummies*, 169.

22. "Calcium Absorption—Bioavailability and Solubility," AlgaeCal.com, http://www.algaecal.com/calcium-absorption.html (accessed July 6, 2009).

23. National Cancer Institute Fact Sheet, "Calcium and Cancer Prevention: Strengths and Limits of the Evidence," Cancer.gov, http://www.cancer.gov/cancertopics/factsheet/prevention/calcium (accessed July 6, 2009).

24. "Calcium Absorption—Bioavailability and Solubility."

25. Mark Percival, "Coral Calcium: Debunking the Debunking!" *The American Chiropractor* (September/October 2003) 38–39.

26. "Study: Some Acid Reflux Drugs Raise Risk of Hip Fractures," FOXNews.com, http://www.foxnews.com/printer_friendly_story/0,3566,523957,00.html (accessed August 4, 2009).

Don Colbert, MD, was born in Tupelo, Mississippi. He attended Oral Roberts School of Medicine in Tulsa, Oklahoma, where he received a bachelor of science degree in biology in addition to his degree in medicine. Dr. Colbert completed his internship and residency with Florida Hospital in Orlando, Florida. He is board certified in family practice and anti-aging medicine and has received extensive training in nutritional medicine.

If you would like more
information about natural and
divine healing, or information about
Divine Health nutritional products,
you may contact Dr. Colbert at:

Don Colbert, MD

1908 Boothe Circle
Longwood, FL 32750
Telephone: 407-331-7007 (for ordering product only)
Dr. Colbert's Web site is
www.drcolbert.com.

Disclaimer: Dr. Colbert and the staff of Divine Health Wellness Center are prohibited from addressing a patient's medical condition by phone, facsimile, or e-mail. Please refer questions related to your medical condition to your own primary care physician.

Pick up these other great Bible Cure books by Don Colbert, MD:

The Bible Cure for ADD and Hyperactivity

The Bible Cure for Allergies

The Bible Cure for Arthritis

The Bible Cure for Asthma

The Bible Cure for Autoimmune Diseases

The Bible Cure for Back Pain

The Bible Cure for Cancer

The Bible Cure for Candida and Yeast Infections

The Bible Cure for Chronic Fatigue and Fibromyalgia

The Bible Cure for Colds, Flu, and Sinus Infections

The Bible Cure for Headaches

The Bible Cure for Heart Disease

The Bible Cure for Heartburn and Indigestion

The Bible Cure for Hepatitis and Hepatitis C

The Bible Cure for High Blood Pressure

The Bible Cure for High Cholesterol

The Bible Cure for Irritable Bowel Syndrome

The Bible Cure for Memory Loss

The Bible Cure for Menopause

The Bible Cure for PMS and Mood Swings

The Bible Cure for Prostate Disorders

The Bible Cure for Skin Disorders

The Bible Cure for Stress

The Bible Cure for Thyroid Disorders

The Bible Cure for Weight Loss and Muscle Gain

The Bible Cure Recipes for Overcoming Candida

The New Bible Cure for Depression and Anxiety

The New Bible Cure for Diabetes

The New Bible Cure for Sleep Disorders